AIRSHIP

AIRSHIP

The story of R.34

Patrick Abbott

BREWIN BOOKS

First published
by Brewin Books, Studley, Warwickshire, B80 7LG
in May 1994

By the same Author

Family Patterns (published 1971)
Airship (Published 1973)
The British Airship at War (Published 1989)
Airships (Published 1991)

ISBN 1 85858 020 X

British Library Cataloguing in Publication Data.
A Catalogue record for this book is available from the British Library

Typeset in Times by Avon Dataset, Bidford on Avon, Warwickshire, B50 4JH
Printed and bound by WBC, Bridgend, Mid Glam.

Preface

All history is based ultimately on memory; and memory may be as fallible after five minutes as after half a century. This book is based as far as possible on contemporary accounts and documents, but to these have been added the testimony and recollections of participants who survive fifty years after the event. Even contemporary versions of the story presented here sometimes conflict in details, and often the memory of one person cannot be checked against another source. But to write a story which took no cognizance of unsupported evidence would be to write a rather tedious report, and this has not been my intention. Nearly all the incidents and facts in this book have been recounted by some-one and those few which have no positive authority are deduced from such evidence as is available. Nothing imaginative or hypothetical has been included, and where versions differ, I have chosen that which seems most probable. The story is presented throughout as a straightforward narrative that endeavours to give both airship and crew the long overdue credit and honour to which they are entitled.

My thanks are due to many people who have helped with reminiscences or information, and I am especially grateful to Mrs Hilda Pritchard, Major-General J. D. Shotter, Mr F. P. Browdie and Squadron-Leader J. Forteath. Others who have helped are Mrs O. O'Riordan, Lord Ventry, Flight-Lieutenant W. W. Ballantyne, Messrs. H. Howe-Double, W. Johnson and A. Wedderburn, Commander W. E. May and Captain T. B. Williams. I must also record my gratitude to Mr A. W. L. Nayler of the Royal Aeronautical Society for his exemplary patience and hospitality.

Patrick Abbott   **1973**

Preface to Second Edition

The chance to rewrite my book after the lapse of more than twenty years has given me the opportunity to incorporate many items of information which came along too late for the first edition. Among these are two contemporary reports written by Major Pritchard, an article dealing with the stay in New York from the American perspective, and a page from the airship's log book which has now reappeared. I have taken the opportunity to delete the original chapters dealing with balloons and the early history of airships and to combine in one chapter a brief history with a technical exposition. I have also corrected various errors and tried to provide a better picture of the wartime British airship policy of which R.34 was the culmination. In addition, I have totally revised my original pessimistic remarks about the future of airships; I am pleased to have been proved so wrong! I must again record my sincere thanks to the individuals and institution mentioned above, as well to the Fleet Air Arm Museum, the Museum of Flight at East Fortune, the Imperial War Museum, the Science Museum, the Royal Air Force Museum at Hendon and the Friends of Cardington Airship Station. In particular, I must thank Tom Jamison, Graham Mottram, John Page, Norman Peake, Douglas Robinson and Nick Walmsley for their encouragement and help. Above all, I must thank my wife, Dorothy, who has learned far more about R.34 over the last quarter century than she ever wished to know.

Patrick Abbott   **1994**

Contents

List of Chapters

CHAPTER 1

History and Principles

This book tells the story of an airship, the British R.34, which in 1919 flew from Britain to New York and back, so completing the first east-west flight of the Atlantic, the first double air crossing and the first crossing by a dirigible. The outward flight was the first directly between the United Kingdom and the United States and was also a world endurance record. As with all such achievements, its worth must be judged against the background of contemporary technology.

Airships, also known as dirigibles, are flying machines that are lifted by a buoyant gas, but propelled by engines. To perform efficiently, they must be streamlined and of light construction, adequately powered and readily controlled. In order to comply with these criteria, three types of airship were evolved.

The first of these is known as a 'non-rigid' airship or 'blimp', and typically has a car, containing engine, accommodation and equipment, suspended by rigging from a streamlined fabric gasbag or 'envelope', which is kept firm and taut by having smaller internal bags, called 'ballonets', into which air is forced as required, to maintain the pressure. Vertical and horizontal stabilising fins are attached to the rear of the envelope and these incorporate rudders for steering and elevators to control the attitude. The trim may be altered by moving the centres of lift or gravity in some manner and the buoyancy regulated by releasing water ballast or gas. These craft originated in 1784, barely a year after the first balloons flew successfully, when Jean Meusnier of France drew up plans for an airship that was never constructed, for lack of a suitable engine. During the next century, for the same reason, little real progress was made, although in 1852 Henri Giffard made a flight of sorts in his steam-powered airship, and in 1884 Renards and Krebs made the first ever circular flight in their electric-powered craft. Some years later, the lightweight petrol engine at last appeared and it was first used to power an airship by a German, Wolfert, in 1897. Unhappily, the lack of a safe ignition system caused the craft to catch fire and crash, killing the inventor instantly.

Not long afterwards, a safer ignition method was developed and this enabled Alberto Santos Dumont to become the real inventor of the non-rigid airship. His series of small dirigibles made many controlled flights, of which the most famous was in 1901, when he won the Deutsch Prize by flying from St. Cloud to the centre of Paris, rounding the Eiffel Tower and returning safely to his starting place, all within half an hour.

Following his lead, inventors all over Europe began to produce dirigibles to the same basic pattern and in the years leading up to the Great War, they became steadily faster and more efficient. In Britain the foremost pioneer was Ernest Willows, who made the first airship flight from Britain to France. The Army also produced its own series of small blimps for scouting purposes, of which the best known was *Beta*, which flew many hours in service and survived long enough to play a small part in the opening events of the First World War.

Non-rigids were built throughout this century and there are still many flying today in all parts of the world.

As development proceeded, dirigibles were inevitably made larger, in order to benefit from the inescapable mathematical rule that as any given shape increases in size, its surface area increases as the square of the linear dimensions, but its volume increases as the cube. This means that as airships become bigger, their lift increases much faster than the drag. A dirigible 300 ft long, for example, has 9 times the drag but 27 times the lift of another airship of similar shape that is only 100 ft long, other things being equal. Unfortunately, in practice, there is a limit to the size a non-rigid airship can reach, beyond which ballonets alone cannot maintain sufficient pressure to keep the envelope from losing shape and buckling. In an endeavour to solve this problem, two other forms of airship were evolved: the 'semi-rigid' and the 'rigid'.

The first of these are airships very similar to non-rigids, but in addition to the normal features, their envelopes are stiffened by some form of keel stretching at the base from bow to stern. Rigging lines are often positioned internally and cars can be attached directly to the keel. The first successful semi-rigid was made by the Lebaudy brothers of France in 1902, but most of the later types came from Italy. Britain's first military airship, the *Nulli Secundus*, flew originally as a non-rigid but was subsequently converted into a semi-rigid: one of only two built in this country. Another was purchased from Italy by the Admiralty in 1918.

No semi-rigids have been made anywhere in the world for many years.

The final, and most sophisticated, form of airship is the 'rigid', which normally consists of a streamlined framework or 'hull' of lightweight girders, the whole covered by fabric and containing perhaps a score of separate gasbags as well as extra space for crew and equipment. No matter how much gas is lost, this type of airship still retains its shape unaltered. The engines are generally placed in cars slung below the hull and the girders are usually of duralumin, although wood has also been used successfully.

The rigid airship was invented and developed almost entirely by one man and one country: Count Ferdinand von Zeppelin and Germany. His first two airships showed promise, but his third, LZ.3, which first flew in 1906, was wholly successful. Improved versions soon followed and they proved to be far more efficient than any of the other airships flying elsewhere in Europe. In the years leading up to the First World War, they became increasingly bigger, more reliable and more frightening to other nations, for although used with conspicuous success to carry passengers in peaceful comfort and safety, it was the potential of 'zeppelins' as bombing machines which obsessed many military men on both sides of the divide. So worried was the British Government, that a rigid airship was ordered from the firm of Vickers, to be based on what could be learned of German practice. It was designated His Majesty's Airship No.1 and was delivered to the Admiralty in 1911, but was wrecked due to bad handling before it could make even a test flight. At about the same time, the French made a similar craft, but this also proved a failure and was soon broken up. No other attempts outside Germany were made before the war to build a rigid airship but in later years nearly a score were produced by Britain and the United States.

The last traditional type of rigid airship ever to fly was LZ.130, a sister ship to the *Hindenburg,* which was dismantled in 1940.

Despite their differences, all three types of airship share the same basic attributes, features and failings. They use hydrogen or helium, although the latter, which does not burn and is thus much safer, is slightly heavier and has become available outside America only since the Second World War. Hydrogen, which is inflammable by itself and explosive when contaminated by air, is the lightest of all gases and is readily available. The lift it provides depends upon the weight of air which is displaced, minus the weight of the gas displacing it. At sea-level, normal air weighs about 75 lb for 1,000 cubic ft, while the same volume of hydrogen weighs around 5 lb, so giving some 70 lb of lift. In realistic terms, 32,000 cubic ft of hydrogen will lift about 1 ton, so an airship of 320,000 cubic ft capacity, for example, will possess a 'gross lift' of about 10 tons, from which is subtracted the weight of the permanent structure to give the amount of 'disposable lift' or 'useful lift' available for crew, ballast, fuel and payload. However, the exact degree of lift is influenced by many other factors. Air pressure decreases with altitude, so as an airship climbs, the gas inside expands equally and the speed of ascent remains constant. When the gasbags become full, the 'pressure height' is reached and the gas is forced out through automatic valves. The rate of ascent then slackens and at the airship's 'ceiling', stops completely. When a dirigible descends, the process happens in reverse and the gas contracts.

Ambient weather conditions constantly affect an airship in flight and the enclosed gas responds more strongly than does the surrounding air. Sunlight causes 'superheating', when the gas becomes warmer than the air and expands to give 'false lift', so causing the airship to rise. The same effect is experienced when a region of cold air is encountered suddenly. There is also the opposite phenomenon of 'supercooling', which occurs usually at night or when warm air is encountered. The gas has a lower temperature than the outside air and there is 'latent lift' as the airship sinks. Nevertheless, provided the airship is on the ground, the best time for lift is normally at night, when air density is at its highest. The gasbags are topped up as the gas contracts, so although the weight of the gas is more than by day, the total weight of air displaced is even greater.

Although lift is needed to leave the ground, once airborne, a dirigible should ideally fly in a state of equilibrium, neither ascending nor descending. The elevators can then be used to change the attitude and so send the airship up or down anywhere below pressure height. Alternatively, the trim can be altered by moving the centres of lift or gravity in some way and so achieving the same result. In practice, it is almost impossible for an airship not to be slightly light or heavy, but it is not necessary always to be sacrificing valuable gas or ballast to correct this, for dirigibles of all types possess an additional source of lift. If an airship is flown in a nose-up attitude, then not only is the thrust line of the propellers inclined, but the whole envelope or hull acts in the same manner as an aeroplane's wing and gives 'dynamic lift'. Not only can this force compensate for extra weight or the loss of 'static lift', but it can also operate in reverse, to reduce lift, so enabling the airship to climb, dive or maintain a constant height for long periods by using only the elevators, or by altering the trim. Of course, at low speeds, such dynamic forces are very weak and airships have to be handled with care when slowing for landing, because of the consequent loss of controllability. In an attempt to overcome this handicap, airships have sometimes been equipped with propellers that swivel to push the craft upward or downward. Compared with aeroplanes, all airships are slow and fragile, and their large surface area combines with their buoyancy and light construction to make them very vulnerable to wind when on the ground. They cannot normally land or take-off unaided and require a numerous ground crew to handle them safely in or out of the large and expensive hangars which must be provided, even when mooring towers are also available. And until helium became available, there was always the risk of fire to be added to the hazard of bad weather. Nevertheless, during the early part of this century, airships were only slightly slower than aeroplanes and commonly possessed the advantages of being able to fly in poor conditions, to carry out repairs during flight, to remain aloft for long periods and to carry a large load of men, bombs, equipment or fuel. For many duties they were far more suitable than aeroplanes, which were generally small, unreliable and with a restricted range. The First World War was the golden age of the airship.

LZ.3, the world's first really successful rigid airship. (Luftschiffbau Zeppelin)

CHAPTER 2

War in the Air

When the First World War began, on 4 August 1914, Germany possessed only seven military zeppelins: six belonging to the army and one to the navy. But unlike the Allies, the Germans had a wealth of experience and technical expertise to draw upon, and it was soon to be mobilised with deadly effect as they began to build rigid airships in ever increasing numbers, each an improvement on the one before. During the four years of the war the Zeppelin Company produced nearly a hundred, and another firm, Schütte-Lanz, whose airships were wooden-framed, added several more. Even before they were commissioned, these huge monsters inspired a panic in their opponents out of all proportion to their actual potentiality for inflicting destruction and they were feared by the civilian population far more than the much deadlier bombers of the Second World War.

It was on 19 January 1915, that the first zeppelin raid on England took place, and between then and 5 August 1918, when the last airship attack on Britain ended with the shooting down of L.70, zeppelins continued to bring trouble to industry and fear to the populace. Slowly, however, the invincible zeppelins found their dominance being threatened. Aeroplanes, cheaper to construct and easier to develop, began to improve from their first position of inferiority and to combine effective armament with high performance. Anti-aircraft guns were positioned to ring the big cities and incendiary bullets came into use. These measures did not go unanswered, for the German designers met the challenge with skill, contriving to wring a small improvement out of each successive model. Most of the airships were controlled by the Navy, as in Britain, and the classification of these naval zeppelins shows their design development. They were consecutively numbered and divided into classes, the first airship in each giving its number also to the class. Each class was a development of the previous one and each individual airship also incorporated minor improvements, so that there was a continual, if gradual, advance in design.

Up to 1916 the various classes were all basically similar, but in that year the L.20 class came to an end with L.24 and there was a hiatus before the L.30 class appeared. These became known in Britain as 'super-zeppelins' and were much larger than any earlier dirigible, with a capacity of 1,950,000 cubic ft. Designed as an answer to the improved aeroplanes and anti-aircraft guns which had appeared since 1914, they had an extended range and endurance. More engine power gave an improved performance and a ceiling of 14,000 ft was intended to lift them beyond the reach of fighter aeroplanes. The most obvious change from previous zeppelins was shown in the shape of the hull. Hitherto, this had usually been long and slim, with nearly identical bows and stern, and a constant diameter over most of the length. A more streamlined form had been used for some time by the rival firm of Schutte-Lanz and a modified version of this was now adopted by the Zeppelin Company. Smoother curves, a more gradual taper towards the stern, a much

5

L.32 was the third of the German 'super-zeppelins' on which the design of R.34 was based. This airship accompanied L.33 to England on 24 September 1916 and was shot down with the loss of all on board. (Deutsches Museum)

shorter parallel portion and simpler tail surfaces were the main features of the new design. Not only was this shape better in aerodynamic terms, but it produced a far more graceful outline, adding strength to the old engineering dictum that what looks right, must be right.

In 1917, the L.42 'height climber' class came into being by a modification and lightening of the L.30 design. Intended to fly at over 20,000 ft, these ships imposed a considerable strain on their crews because of the lack of heating and proper oxygen equipment. The high ceiling, when it was scrupulously maintained, kept the airships relatively safe from attack, but its effect on German navigation and bomb-aiming — never very accurate at any time — was to make the destruction of military targets even more a matter of luck. The British Government made a practice of revealing few details of the actual damage sustained and it was probably this lack of certain information that led the Germans to overestimate the effect of the raids. Consequently, they chose to persevere with these rather than divert their efforts to long-range sea reconnaissance, where they might have achieved devastating results by combining with submarines to intercept Allied convoys.

Finally, in 1918, came the L.70 'long range' class, created by lengthening the basic L.30 frame in order to enclose extra gasbags. The largest of these ships was 743 ft long and probably capable of staying aloft for more than five days. They were the last and finest of all fighting airships and the Germans later boasted that they would have been capable of bombing New York.

All this brilliance, however, could not prevent the gradual realisation that the zeppelin was no longer an economically viable weapon, if it ever had been. The raids on Britain had certainly frightened people and caused material damage, but even at the beginning, it is doubtful whether this return was worth the risk of losing costly ships and highly skilled men. Very soon, the risk became almost a certainty, for all the development of which the German engineers were capable could not remove the Achilles' heel of the zeppelin.

Helium was unobtainable outside America and hydrogen could never be anything other than highly inflammable. Even as early as June 1915, a British pilot pursued a zeppelin which had strayed off course, caught it up over Belgium and dropped several small bombs directly into the unprotected gasbags. They were enough. In moments the unwieldy titan plunged flaming to destruction, the first of many to perish in similar fashion. One of the very few men to live through the flaring horror of a later zeppelin crash — that of L.48 —

survived to tell a terrible story. His account of the long, five-minute fall to earth, the screams of men burning alive and the helpless despair of those trapped in the control-car, was a frightful reminder of the one fear that never left the minds of even the bravest German airman. For this immediate inflammability was something against which no care, no bravery and no skill could guard. Although a production rate of a new airship every fortnight was maintained through much of the war, when the Armistice came to be signed, fewer than a dozen zeppelins were in active use. In retrospect, it seems likely that had peace not intervened, the use of fighting airships would soon have been discontinued. Nevertheless, the wartime history of the large rigids was not all a chronicle of failure and even in England there were many people who still believed in their value. One of the occasions when they had appeared to vindicate themselves was at the Battle of Jutland. Whether their presence had any real effect on the outcome is now considered doubtful, but a popular contemporary theory in England held that their use had enabled the German fleet to escape. Partisans of the airship seized upon this feeling and urged once more the merits of the rigid dirigible.

The British Government had already shown some tardy interest and in January 1914, the four Army blimps were taken over by the Admiralty, which assumed responsibility for all airships. At the outbreak of war, seven were in service, of which No.2 was a Willows, No.3 a French Astra Torres and No.4 a German Parseval. Together they formed the Airship Service, which was a branch of the Royal Naval Air Service and was led by Wing Commander A.E.D.Masterman. Within a year, however, native airships were being built in large numbers and a chain of airship stations had been established around the British coasts. None was more than a hundred miles from its neighbour and many soon had large hangars capable of housing the biggest airship. In sharp contrast to the German airships, however, the British dirigibles were nearly all small, crude and cheap. But in equally sharp

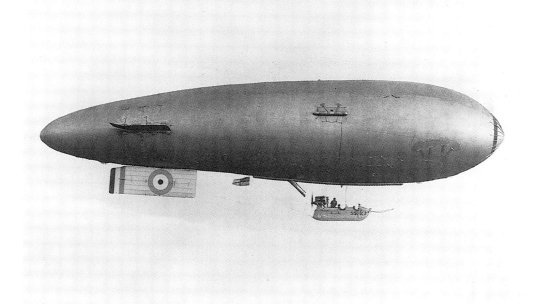

An SS Zero non-rigid airship of 1917. (Fleet Air Arm Museum)

7

His Majesty's Airship No. 9 was the first British rigid to fly successfully. The outdated form of her hull compares unfavourably with that of the streamlined L.32, a contemporary German airship.
(Fleet Air Arm Museum)

contrast, they were not wasted on suicidal bombing missions over enemy territory, but were deployed at sea, where their virtues of long range and endurance proved invaluable in the crucial battle against the U-boats. The strategy was based on the limitations which already affected their opponents, for the U-boats were unable to advance far into the Atlantic and attacked shipping only in British waters. Unlike aeroplanes, the airships could match the submarines for range and they patrolled the seas, escorted convoys and sought for signs of the enemy. Each airship carried her own W.T. (Wireless Telegraphy) operator, who periodically transmitted the ship's call sign. The captain was then regularly informed of his exact position, calculated by wireless stations on land using bearings obtained by D.F.W.T. (Direction Finding Wireless Telegraphy).

There were many signs to indicate the possible presence of a submarine, from the wake of a periscope to floating oil leaked from propeller shafts, and these could be detected from the air more readily and more widely than from a surface vessel. Although all airships were armed with bombs and joined in attacks, their prime function was to find the U-boats and then to summon armed merchantmen or destroyers to the exact location. The airships could operate with impunity, for not only were the U-boats unable to strike back without surfacing and so becoming immediately vulnerable to any warship, but the German aeroplanes, which could otherwise have protected them, were stationed too far away and did not possess the range necessary to intervene. During the whole course of the war, the only British airships that were destroyed by enemy aeroplanes were two Coastals, both of which had unfortunately strayed too close to the German coast. The zeppelins, which could have intervened effectively, were surprisingly never used in support of the U-boats and no direct combat between airships ever took place.

The wartime record of the British Airship Service is one of very effective defence and deterrence; on only one occasion was a ship sunk by a U-boat while being escorted, and — again in a most telling contrast to Germany — by the end of the war more than a hundred airships were in service. Over two million miles had been flown in service at a cost of fewer than fifty lives.

The first of the British wartime airships were the SS or Submarine Scout class. To start with, each of these was made by slinging an aeroplane fuselage beneath an improvised gasbag, adding wireless and bombs, and considerably increasing the fuel capacity. Development proceeded throughout the war, however, as larger and more efficient versions appeared. The most successful were the famous Zero airships, each of 80,000 cubic ft capacity. They carried a pilot, an engineer and a wireless operator who was also a gunner when required. More than seventy of these blimps were made altogether and although the first entered the war only in 1917, several flew more than a thousand hours in service.

In an attempt to produce a larger airship, which would carry more men, fuel and bombs, the Coastal class appeared in 1916 and featured the tri-lobe envelope, with partly internal rigging, which had been pioneered by the French Astra Torres firm. The car, which was basically two aeroplane fuselages cut short and fastened together end to end, carried two engines for greater reliability. More than thirty Coastals, each with a capacity of 170,000 cubic ft and a length of 196 ft, were built and they saw more action than any other type of British airship. One of them, C.9, flew a record 2,500 hours in service, two were shot down, four were sold to Russia, one was bought by France and another was confiscated by the Dutch government when it made a forced landing in Holland.

The Coastals were followed by the C.Star class, which were basically enlarged, improved and more streamlined versions of their predecessors, and by the North Sea class, which appeared towards the end of the war. After early problems over engine transmission had been overcome, these last proved to be excellent airships, with enclosed cabins, a length of 260 ft and a capacity of 360,000 cubic ft, which gave them a disposable lift of 3.8 tons and the ability to remain aloft for long periods. In February 1919, NS.11 set a world endurance record of 100 hours 50 minutes. Sadly, five months later, the same ship was struck by lightning and destroyed with all on board.

But while the non-rigid type of airship was so successful, the rigid was at first neglected by the Admiralty, deterred by the failure of No.1, three years before the war. However, in June 1913, an order was given to Vickers to build a rigid airship designated No.9. She was to be based on German practice and the information which had been obtained when the German Army Z.4 had accidentally landed at Luneville in France. Work began in 1914, but the project was abandoned early in the following year, only to be reinstated in the August. More than simply time had been lost, however, and it was not until 1917 that the new rigid was at last delivered to the Royal Naval Air Service. She was 526 ft long overall, with a total capacity of 846,000 cubic ft and a speed of less than 45 m.p.h. Despite intensive modification and lightening, she had a disposable lift of only 3.8 tons: the same as that of a North Sea blimp. Because she was now so old-fashioned, the Admiralty restricted her to experimental and training work and only one ocean patrol was carried out, on 21/22 July, when Flight Lieutenant G. H. Scott captained her on an uneventful cruise of 26 hours 45 minutes over the North Sea.

Although No.9 was deleted before the end of the war, her design formed the basis of the four airships of the 23 class: No.23, No.24, No.25 and R.26 (the first to use the prefix R). These were an improvement on No.9, having lengthened and modified hulls to produce extra lift and more engine-power to increase speed. Each was 535 ft long with a capacity of

942,000 cubic ft and a disposable lift of about 6.5 tons. None achieved any great distinction and all four were deleted in 1919.

The next class became known as the 23X class and was intended to consist of four airships designated R.27, R.28, R.29 and R.30. These were to be developments of the 23 class, each having a length of 539 ft and a capacity of 990,000 cubic ft. They had a redesigned hull, but the principal difference from their predecessors was the elimination of the external keel corridor, which increased the disposable lift to 8.5 tons and also improved the steering. Only two of these ships were actually built: R.27 and R.29. The former was destroyed in an accidental fire at Howden in August 1918, but the latter proved to be the best of all the wartime rigids and survived until deleted in October 1919.

In addition to these seven, there were also the two rigid airships of the 31 class, which were based on the Schutte-Lanz dirigibles and used a hull framework of wood. The first was R.31, 615 ft long and with a capacity of 1,500,000 cubic ft. She was delivered just before the Armistice and was found to have the outstanding top speed of some 70 m.p.h. before modifications that reduced her power but increased her disposable lift to nearly twenty tons. Unfortunately, she proved to have been faultily constructed, and flew only a few hours before being grounded. She then slowly fell to pieces and was eventually officially deleted in July 1919. Her sister ship, R.32, was more successful, but she was not delivered until September 1919 and survived only two years before deletion. All these rigid airships, except No.9, used Rolls Royce engines, which were the best and most reliable then available. Unlike the earlier situation at the beginning of the war, no expense was now spared and the drive to build these rigids seems to have become a matter of national prestige, rather than a rational exercise, for they were at once both far more expensive and far less effective than the humble non-rigids. They were used mainly for training and experimental purposes and they contributed very little directly to the war effort. R.29 became the only British rigid ever to see action when she joined with warships to bomb and destroy an enemy U-boat in September 1918.

Nevertheless, the Admiralty persevered with the rigid airship programme, although it was clear that these native rigid airships were very inferior to their German counterparts. In their efforts to draw level with the enemy, the British designers would gladly have taken a short cut and, just as English sloops of the Napoleonic era were based on the French ship, *Amazon*, so all wrecked zeppelins were examined closely for their secrets. Inevitably, most of them were burned beyond the point of providing useful information, and despoliation and looting were an additional hazard.

But in the autumn of 1916, three new zeppelins of the L.30 class attacked London, two of them by way of Kent and the third from the east. Of these three, L.31 reached home again safely — only to be destroyed on her next raid — and L.32 was shot down over Burstead with the loss of all on board. The third ship, L.33, commanded by Kapitanleutnant Boecker, dropped her bombs over West Ham, where she came under fire from the anti-aircraft batteries. One shell exploded in the forepart of the hull but the gas somehow failed to catch fire and the airship was able to make her escape north-eastwards towards Chelmsford. Here she was intercepted by Lieutenant Brandon, patrolling the area in a B.E.2c biplane, and he came in at once to the attack, raking the towering flanks of the zeppelin again and again with his machine gun until the frail gasbags were riddled and torn. Boecker strove in vain to evade or repel his persistent opponent, for the ship was handling sluggishly and his gunners dared not fire back at their tormentor for fear of igniting the hydrogen now leaking fast all around them from the numerous rents and gashes. Despite

Brandon's efforts, the gas still miraculously refused to burn, and when his gun jammed he was obliged to break off the fight and let the zeppelin disappear into the protecting darkness. But the airman had wrought better than he knew, for L.33 was in a parlous state, sinking slowly towards the ground with her precious buoyancy ebbing remorselessly away. Kapitanleutnant Boecker drove his ship forward with her nose pointing towards the moonless sky while his men despairingly jettisoned ballast, fuel, ammunition and anything else they could handle or prise loose. It was to no avail and at some time in the early hours of 24 September, the crippled ship settled down gently in a lonely field, not far from Little Wigborough in Essex, with her gas exhausted, her fabric in tatters, but her main structure almost unharmed. Not one of the crew was seriously injured and they tumbled out of their stranded craft to stand firmly on British soil, the only armed and disciplined group of invaders to do so during the whole course of the war. Then, with some faint hope of avoiding the indignity and frustration of captivity, they set off for the coast, to search for a boat that might carry them across the North Sea. Before they left, Boecker set fire to the abandoned airship, which burned fitfully behind them as they marched in step down the narrow lanes. Neither crew nor airship escaped from the English, however, as the fire in the airship expired for lack of fuel and the weary airshipmen soon surrendered themselves to the solitary special constable on a bicycle who rode up and confronted them.

Before very long, the crew were prisoners, the ship cordoned off, and the Admiralty informed that the nearly intact specimen they had coveted was now available. Crowds flocked from London to stare in awe at the prostrate giant, and a team from the Admiralty, led by C.I.R. Campbell swarmed over the framework, inspecting, measuring and making drawings. Public interest was intense and even such preoccupied statesmen as Lloyd George and Balfour found time to travel to Essex and satisfy their curiosity. So impressed by their findings were the investigators and so plausible was their report, that the Admiralty eventually decided that although most of the native rigids already planned should be completed, no more would be ordered and both R.28 and R.30 would be cancelled. Quite evidently the German airship had proved to be far in advance of anything the British engineers could yet contemplate, and the Admiralty ordered that replicas of L.33, only slightly modified, should be constructed for British use. A fleet of seventeen seems to have been the provisional estimate, with the designation numbers running probably from R.33 to R.49. but, in the event, only two were constructed. The first of these, R.33, repeating the number of her alien prototype by coincidence only, was built by Armstrong Whitworth and had a long career. Finally demolished in 1928 after about 800 hours of flying, she was an unsung paragon and the longest lasting of all the early British airships.

Her sister ship, R.34, complemented this achievement by becoming the most famous.

R34. CONTROL CAR.

Contemporary artist's impression of R.34's control car. (Aeronautics)

CHAPTER 3

Design of R.34

To the members of her crew, His Majesty's Airship R.34 was known as 'Tiny' — inevitably. For she was enormous: as big as a contemporary 'Dreadnought' battleship and far larger than any aeroplane which has ever flown. Her overall length from bow to stern was 643 ft, twice as long as a football field; her maximum diameter was 79 ft and her overall height just short of 92 ft. Her cost was around £350,000 and her total gas capacity was 1,950,000 cubic ft, giving a gross lift of about 59 tons and a disposable lift, when the weight of the structure and permanent fittings was discounted, of supposedly 26 tons. She was intended to cruise at 45 m.p.h., with a maximum speed of 62 m.p.h. In practice, even these modest estimates proved somewhat optimistic and R.34 probably never carried a load much above 24 tons or reached an airspeed in excess of 56 m.p.h., although R.33 — of identical design — was once officially timed at 60 m.p.h.

Five engines were fitted, each of a nominal 250 h.p., making a total power-output considerably less than that of many single-seater fighter aeroplanes of the Second World War. A close watch had been kept on German technical development and R.34, in one important particular, had departed from the engine plan of L.33 to follow instead that of the later and more advanced L.49, which had been forced to land in France in October 1917. The former ship had boasted six engines: one to each of the three forward propellers, one to the rear propeller and two driving small 'wing' propellers by shaft. On the latter vessel, the designers had done away with this cumbersome arrangement, eliminating one engine and the two wing propellers entirely, and harnessing the power of two rear engines to a single enlarged propeller. This was the system which was now adopted for R.34.

The framework of the airship was constructed mainly of slim triangular-section girders formed of narrow duralumin channel, the three running members braced together by diagonals. The hull so formed had the cross-section of a twenty-five sided polygon. Twenty main circumferential girder frames, each of thirteen sides, were spaced regularly throughout the length, 32 ft apart and interspersed by auxiliary circumferential frames of lighter construction. At each of the main frames, radial steel wires led to a central axial plate, like the spokes of a bicycle wheel, and each plate was joined to the next by a wire stay. All of these last connected up to form, in effect, a single axial cable running from end to end of the ship to provide lengthwise bracing. At right angles to these transverse frames, attached at each corner, were thirteen main longitudinal girders which were interspersed, except for the lowest two, by intermediate longitudinal girders. This whole framework was varnished to prevent atmospheric corrosion and heavily braced by wiring. In the case of the main longitudinal girders, this wiring ran diagonally from the corners made with the main circumferential frames, while the intermediate girders were similarly cross-wired to the auxiliary transverse frames. These wires were termed major and minor diagonals

13

R.34 under construction in the Beardmore factory at Inchinnan. The flat surface formed at the bottom of a partially deflated gasbag may be clearly seen. (Flight)

respectively. Lengths of linen fabric were stretched between each pair of frames, to which they were attached by laces. Narrow strips were then glued over the lacing and the whole covering of the hull was painted with dope containing aluminium powder, to reflect the sunlight and so reduce superheating.

At the extreme stern was a cross-shaped frame known as the cruciform girder. This supported the vertical and horizontal tail fins, which were similarly shaped, braced by wire rigging and incorporated the twin rudders and twin elevators respectively. Each of these moved through a maximum of twenty degrees on either side of the mid-position and each could be operated independently of its partner if required. Additionally, the elevators could be locked in the level position to facilitate running repairs. Like the hull, the fins were constructed of duralumin girders and covered with linen fabric. The cloth itself was manufactured in Belfast to special order; woven extremely fine, it was of such excellent quality that spare portions found their way to some unexpected uses. Miss Olga Buckley, the fiancée of the Second Officer, Captain Greenland, was probably not the only young lady to receive a present of several yards with which to prepare her trousseau.

R.34 at a later stage of construction. The outer cover is being laced into position before the sealing strips are glued on. (Flight)

In the chambers formed by the main circumferential frames and the longitudinal girders were the gasbags, nineteen in all and made of one thickness of rubber-proofed cotton cloth, varnished and lined with goldbeaters' skins. (This unlikely material is the outside membrane of the large intestine of an ox, and is more impervious to gas than almost any other substance of similar weight. Some 600,000 separate skins, from as many animals, were required for R.34.) Each gasbag was contoured to fill all the available space and was surrounded by cord mesh to prevent chafing against the girders. Each possessed an automatic release valve — to cope with expansion of the gas caused by height or heat — and these discharged from near the base into an exhaust shaft between each pair of gasbags, although that nearest to the bows had one to itself. Eight of these shafts led up to the top of the hull, but the two foremost discharged lower down on either side, so that bullets from a gun on the top platform firing forward would not ignite escaping gas. Nine of the gasbags — Nos. 2, 5, 6, 7, 8, 11, 12, 14 & 15 — also possessed hand-operated valves on top, for use when manoeuvring or landing. A main gas duct led along the starboard side and this enabled the gasbags to be filled either separately or together. Each gasbag had narrow, central sleeves on front and rear, and through these ran the long axial cable connecting the airship's nose and tail.

15

The forward gondola of R.34. The airship is being 'eased up', preparatory to flight, when the lines held by the ground crew will be released from the handling rail. (Royal Aeronautical Society)

Beneath the main body of the airship, suspended by long, wooden struts and braced by rigging wires, were four small cars or gondolas, whose rather angular lines contrasted oddly with the vast silvery-grey streamlining of the hull above them. The forward gondola was some fifty feet long and although to outward appearances a single unit, was actually made up of two parts separated by a narrow gap, intended to prevent vibration from the engine affecting the W.T. equipment. Incorporated in the forward section were a control room and a small wireless cabin, below which, during flight, trailed a long aerial. The control-cabin, which was fronted with 'Triplex' safety glass and had handling rails mounted low on each side, had an internal width of just under six feet, and from its cramped space the captain directed his widely spread command. Here were the steering and elevator wheels, the gas-valve controls, the engine telegraph, the various navigational and other instruments, and the toggles controlling the emergency forward water ballast. Also to hand were a chart table, an Aldis signalling lamp and a variety of minor fittings. Connecting the control-cabin with the keel was a ladder, protected from the elements by a streamlined canvas cover. Another cover similarly enclosed the numerous control-wires and connections that led up into the hull.

In the rear section of the forward gondola was the first of the engines, driving a single 'pusher' propeller 17 ft in diameter. Amidships were the two smaller 'wing' gondolas, each housing an engine together with reversing gear — a refinement that enabled the airship to brake during flight. Incorporated in the starboard engine only was a large flanged plate, welded to the exhaust pipe, on which saucepans or containers might be placed. This was the only method of cooking available on board and it allowed water or liquids to be boiled, although the heat was too great for frying. Further aft, three-quarters of the way to the tail, was the rear or after car. This housed two engines coupled together and driving a larger propeller which measured nearly 20 ft from tip to tip. To the front of these engines was a small space with auxiliary rudder and elevator controls, which could be operated if those in the main control-cabin failed. The rear car was ringed with a rail to assist handlers, and, as with the forward gondola, two 'bumping bags' of compressed air were positioned underneath to help cushion landing shocks.

Each of the five engines was a Sunbeam 'Maori': a new type, designed for the Wolverhampton firm by a Frenchman, Louis Coatalen and intended specifically for airship use, but clearly inferior to the Rolls Royce engines used by earlier British rigids. Unfortunately, no Rolls Royce engines could be made available, as all those produced were now reserved for aeroplane use, and the Sunbeams had been accepted reluctantly. Like most aero engines of that time, they were unreliable, required constant maintenance, frequently broke down, and consumed large amounts of oil. Each engine had twelve water-cooled cylinders, which were intended to produce full power at a theoretical 2,100 r.p.m., although in practice, it was rare for 1,600 r.p.m. to be exceeded. In the forward and wing cars, the radiators were mounted externally and controlled by folding shutters, but the

The two wing gondolas of R.34. (Royal Aeronautical Society)

The after gondola of R.34, containing two engines geared to one propeller. The emergency elevator wheel may be seen through the central window. (Royal Aeronautical Society)

other two, in the after car, could be raised or lowered and fixed in the optimum position, with armoured rubber hosing to provide flexible connections. Each engine was fitted with a hand starter, while the drive to the propellers was through a sliding dog-clutch, a Hele Shaw clutch and a reduction gearbox with a ratio of 1 : 3.86. The clutch enabled the engine to be started and warmed up before flight without incurring danger to the handling-party, and made it easier to carry out repairs in the air. If the engine should be stopped during flight, the disconnected propeller could rotate freely in the airstream to reduce head resistance, although if it was required to remain stationary for landing or any other reason, a special brake was provided for this purpose. Assuming that the airship was still moving forwards, the engine might then be started by releasing the brake and engaging the clutch again.

In addition to the gondolas, a considerable amount of space was available also inside the hull and invisible to the outside observer. Running almost the entire length of the ship was a long keel corridor, consisting of a succession of A-shaped frames standing on the two lowest girders, and with three auxiliary longitudinal girders of their own to fence off the surrounding gasbags. At its widest part, this corridor was about 10 ft across, narrowing somewhat towards the extremities. As the only flooring otherwise was the tautened fabric, another girder was interposed between the two on which the A-frames rested, and this was covered by a plywood cat-walk, known as the 'walking-way'. It was barely a foot wide for most of its length and the only safety measure was a single rope positioned overhead. Anyone stepping off onto the outer cover was likely to fall right through — a disconcerting

The 'walking-way' in the keel of R.34, shown when the airship was still under construction. Some of the aluminium fuel tanks and canvas bags for the water ballast may be seen. (Royal Aeronautical Society)

risk for the crew, especially as their hammocks were slung right above the frail linen.

Access points from the corridor led to the gondolas and to other parts of the hull, whereby the gasbags and structure might be inspected and repaired if necessary. Leading to the wing and after cars were narrow ladders, fully exposed to the force of the elements.

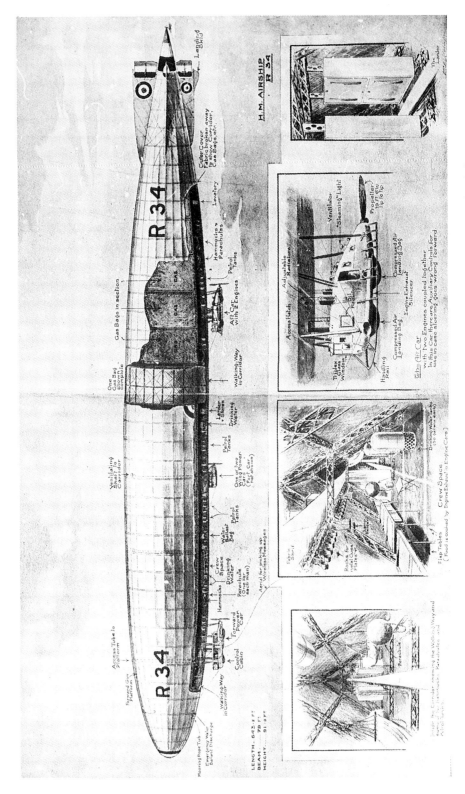

Cutaway drawing of R.34 by W. B. Robinson for Illustrated London News in July 1919.

Two canvas tunnels led off from the corridor. Complete with rope ladder, the first ran vertically upwards from just above the forward car to a machine-gun platform on top of the hull, while the second led similarly to another gun-pit at the stern, immediately abaft the upper tail fin.

Intended not only as a means of communication between the cars, the keel corridor was itself a most important living space and repository for equipment. Hammocks were slung along much of its length, and water-ballast bags, petrol and oil tanks, drinking water, bomb-racks, parachutes and a sea drogue festooned the trellised framework, together with many minor items. Amidships hung the two main ballast bags, each of which held up to about two tons of water that could be released overboard through a canvas tube, as required. At both bows and stern four much smaller bags were hung. These held the emergency ballast and unlike the larger bags, they emptied instantly. Each small bag held a quarter of a ton, so making a total maximum ballast load of about six tons. The ballast at the bows was controlled directly from the control-cabin; that at the tail and amidships was released by a crew member standing in the keel.

The numerous fuel 'slip' tanks were disposed on both sides of the keel and from these the petrol was transferred by means of manually operated semi-rotary pumps to the fixed main tanks above each car, which alone were provided with external gauges. From there it was gravity-fed into smaller tanks and thence by float-control to the engines. All petrol lines were located on one side of the keel, while control and gas-valve wires were placed opposite. At about 200 ft from the bows, the plywood flooring of the walking-way was widened to reach the walls (mesh and gasbags) and this section, 28 ft long, was equipped with fabric shelving, plate-racks and collapsible furniture to form the crew's quarters. A lavatory was situated far aft and the trail rope hatch far forward, directly under the nose. Electric lighting was standard throughout the ship and extended to the cabin instruments whose dials were also picked out with luminous paint. Power for the lights came from accumulators carried in the cars and generators run from the engines.

Finally, there were the various ropes required for the complex handling operations which were necessary when the airship took off, landed or moored. A long trail rope was kept in

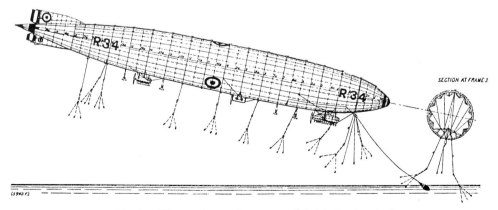

The handling and mooring ropes of R.34. (Engineering)

the keel near the bows, while to the underside of the hull were attached several much shorter handling-guys, which ended in loops. For mooring at sea, a drogue could be attached to the trail rope.

For both the landing and lift-off, there was a prescribed drill which was the same in essence for all airships. Under ideal conditions, the ship finished a flight by halting low over the heads of the landing-party. As the loss of forward motion rendered the elevators ineffective, her lift was carefully adjusted to obtain neutral buoyancy. Then a slight valving of gas brought her gently and slowly within reach of the landing-party — the engines still and the propellers horizontal. They seized the pendent handling-guys, attached lines to the loops and pulled the airship almost to the ground, where the gondolas could be grasped and the ship taken carefully into the hangar. Of course, conditions were seldom ideal and in practice it was usually necessary for the ship to be made positively buoyant. Then she was headed into the wind and the trail rope dropped from its position under the bows. As this struck the ground, it was grabbed by the landing-party who used it to pull the airship down. Sometimes they did this unaided, but more often with the help of a 'snatch-block' — a form of heavy pulley opening at one side, which was set in concrete but swivelled freely. Once a loop of the trail rope was passed under the wheel, the airship could be hauled down easily, without fear of the landing-party being lifted off their feet. Either way, when the ship came low enough, the handling guys were grasped as before and she was taken into the 'shed', as the hangar was usually called. Here she was held down by sandbags and other weights strung at various points, and the guys were tethered at an angle to provide some degree of lateral stability.

The reverse process, by which the airship was prepared for flight, was very similar. She was surrounded by the handling-party who took hold of lines, rails and other handholds. The weights were then cast off and the ship 'walked out', restrained by the weight of perhaps four or five hundred men. Safely outside the hangar confines, she was swung to face into the wind and at the command 'Hands off, ease up the guys', she was allowed to rise to above head height on the handling guys and other lines passed over the rails. If it had not been done already in the hangar, she was then 'ballasted up' or 'weighed off', which meant her buoyancy was adjusted — usually by careful adjustment of the water-ballast or the fuel supply. The amount of lift was assessed by the number of men whose weight, pulling directly on the airship, was enough to bring her down. When all was ready, the engines were started and allowed to warm up. At the word of command — for synchronization was essential; men had been carried to their deaths through holding on too long — the ropes were released and the vessel 'ballooned off'. The lines held by the handling-party slipped from the rails and from the loops of the handling-guys and fell away. The riggers pulled the handling-guys up into the keel, the engine clutches engaged, the propellers took up the drive and the airship was on her way.

When safely in the air, the altitude at which the dirigible flew was regulated by balancing the lift of the gas against the weight of ballast: gas was valved to descend; ballast was released to ascend. In addition to the normal ballast, many of the ship's fuel tanks were slung on slip-attachments so that, in the last resort, they also might be dropped to reduce weight. However, it was not necessary to be continually valving hydrogen or releasing ballast in order to obtain level flight, for like all dirigibles, R.34 possessed considerable dynamic lift which complemented the static lift of the gas and could compensate for any variation of normal conditions caused by rain on the outer cover, supercooling, loss of gas, or any other unexpected contingency. This extra lift depended, of course, on both the angle of the hull and the airspeed. Later experiments on R.33 showed that at an angle of 6 degrees to the horizontal and with a speed of about 45 m.p.h., the lift amounted to about 2.5 tons — a substantial addition to a total disposable lift of 24 tons. At the much lower speed of 32 m.p.h. and flying at an angle of only 1.5 degrees, there was the still appreciable reserve of almost one ton. As these same dynamic forces could also be operated in reverse, to counteract the effects of superheating, consuming fuel, losing weight or gaining buoyancy in any way, it was possible to maintain the airship at the desired height for long periods without the needless waste of ballast or gas.

Depending basically upon the use of her elevators to raise or depress the tail, the attitude taken by the airship could also be changed by altering the centres of gravity or lift in some way. One or more of the water-ballast bags at each end of the ship could be emptied for this purpose, heavy items moved, petrol transferred to other tanks, or hydrogen valved from the appropriate gasbags. The crew themselves also provided a certain amount of easily moved weight, and by sending men forward or aft along the walking-way, the airship's trim could be quickly adjusted.

Other tests on R.33 showed that the turning co-efficient of the two airships was 6.4, giving a minimum turning circle some 4,100 ft in diameter. However, so strong was the effect of the slipstream of the after propeller acting on the rudder, that with the forward engine still and the wing propellers both running in reverse, it was possible to pivot either ship on herself. Lateral stability was considered rather poor, probably because of the relatively small size of the fins, and there was a tendency to yaw, particularly at low speeds, which affected the performance. The vertical stability of both airships was considered excellent.

Although rather slimmer than the theoretical ideal, the aerodynamic shape of R.34 was a distinct improvement on most earlier designs — her total air resistance being only seven per cent of a hypothetical flat disc of the same diameter. In later airships, this was reduced even further, but in her own day the streamlining of R.34 was excellent and twice as effective as that of her British predecessors. This fine streamlining was obviously dependent upon a horizontal attitude being maintained, so that if she flew at an angle, the performance suffered accordingly.

As a peacetime airship, R.34 was never fitted with her full armament. In addition to bomb-racks, the original plan had apparently been to include a ventral 'gun house' abaft the rear car, which would carry a one-pounder Pom-Pom and two Lewis machine guns. Another Lewis gun was to be mounted on the rear platform behind the tail, while six more were to be shared equally among the two wing-cars, the forward gondola and the top gun platform. Nor was this the end of the arsenal, for a two-pounder quick-firing gun was to be placed on each side of the hull and two more were to join the Lewis guns on top. Whether all this heavy armament, which was presumably intended for defence against German zeppelins, could ever have been carried is very doubtful and, in the event, the gun house was never fitted and the number of guns considerably reduced. Only one of R.34's flights could strictly be described as operational: when she was sent to patrol the German Baltic coast before the final signing of the Treaty of Versailles. On this occasion she carried Vickers and Lewis guns on the platforms and in the cars, although their exact disposition is uncertain. No bombs were taken on this or any other flight. However, had there ever been the need, her bomb-load was quite considerable: twenty at 100 lb and four at 550 lb.

The firm of William Beardmore and Company Ltd., of Inchinnan, near Glasgow, began work on R.34 on 9 December 1917 and she was completed just over a year later on 20

December 1918. The designation letter (for 'rigid') and number were painted on both sides of the hull at bow and stern, and the roundels of the Royal Air Force splashed spots of colour on the nose, tail and amidships. With cheerful inconsistency, the White Ensign of the Royal Navy also fluttered at her stern, for at this period all airship personnel were members of the R.A.F., while the airships themselves still belonged to the Admiralty. Like an old-time man-of-war, R.34 also sported a figurehead in the centre of the roundel at her prow: an aluminium shield bearing the rampant lion of Scotland and the motto, 'Pro Patria Volans'. ('Flying for the Motherland')

By the time R.34 was ready for her test flights, the war was over and she was too late for active service. But on 30 December, while bad weather delayed the trial flight, the Admiralty agreed to lend their airships to the Air Ministry for long-distance commercial trials. R.34 was specifically mentioned.

The Royal Arms of Scotland which R.34 carried at her bows. The shield is now on display at East Fortune. (Author's collection)

CHAPTER 4

Race across the Atlantic

In 1909, the early airmen had looked to the English Channel as the testing ground of their primitive machines, and a prize of £1,000 offered by the *Daily Mail* added financial inducement to pioneering zeal. Hubert Latham tried to make the crossing and failed, Louis Blériot succeeded and a year later Charles Rolls made both the first eastward aeroplane flight and also the first double crossing. In the same year, a Clement-Bayard dirigible made the first airship crossing from France to England, while Ernest Willows performed a similar feat in the opposite direction.

Right up to 1914, when the war accelerated aviation out of its infancy, the crossing between England and France continued to command respect and caution. But a little later, in 1919, another measure of their increased ability awaited the challenge of aviators: the wide expanse of the Atlantic. Once again there was an award offered by the *Daily Mail* — this time of £10,000 — for the first direct flight by aeroplane between North America and the British Isles, either way. The contest was far more than a quest for money, however, and even after the prize was finally won, the efforts of the other aviators were only slightly abated.

When the war echoes died away, the contenders began their preparations with aircraft as various as their nationalities. In May 1919, three United States flying boats set out from Newfoundland to fly to Europe by way of the Azores. They enjoyed official backing and a large amount of luck, especially the men of NC-4. Both the other aeroplanes, NC-1 and NC-3, came down in the Atlantic and although the crews suffered no harm, it was Commander Read of NC-4 who finally won through to Portugal and then Plymouth. For the first time ever, an ocean had been crossed by a flying machine, although its crew were not eligible for the *Daily Mail* prize, as the flight had been made in stages.

One of the first attempts on the prize was made by two Britons, Harry Hawker and Kenneth Mackenzie-Grieve, in a single-engined Sopwith biplane. On 18 May, they left Newfoundland on their way to Ireland, jettisoning the undercarriage after take-off in order to reduce weight and air resistance. They disappeared eastwards into fog and silence, and when a week passed without news, they were given up for lost. In fact, their engine had broken down more than 1,000 miles out over the Atlantic and they had been obliged to come down in heavy seas. Incredibly, there was a steamer at hand to rescue them from almost certain death. The ship possessed no radio and so not until several days had passed, when it entered harbour, did the news of the airmen's extraordinary luck become known.

Less than a month later, John Alcock and Arthur Whitten Brown, flying a Vickers Vimy twin-engined biplane, left Newfoundland for Ireland, fame and the *Daily Mail* award. Like all the other competitors, they had chosen the west-to-east route in order that the strong prevailing winds might hurry them forcefully on their way, and their winning flight was comparatively uneventful; the most dangerous moment was probably when the aeroplane nearly turned over on landing. Of aeroplane attempts there were many more, some ending in safety and some in disaster. But it was 1928 before a heavier-than-air craft first flew the Atlantic from east to west, and it was not until 1933 that Amy Johnson and Jim Mollison made the first non-stop aeroplane flight from the United Kingdom to the United States.

Not only aeroplanes had gathered for this venture in 1919, for lighter-than-air craft were also represented, even although they were not strictly eligible for the *Daily Mail* prize. Nor were they the first of their kind, merely the first with any realistic prospects. In 1910, a small airship called *America* had left Atlantic City in a rash attempt to reach Europe. Covering only a few miles under full power before one of the two engines had to be jettisoned as ballast, it had drifted helplessly for many hours until the crew were rescued by a providential steamship. This exploit, brave though it might have been, was premature. Nine years afterwards, all aircraft had improved vastly and there were four dirigibles with more than an outside chance of being the first across.

Quite the most convincing contenders were the two zeppelins, L.71 and L.72, last and best of all the military zeppelins. The Zeppelin Company wished L.72 to make the journey from Germany to New York and back non-stop, as a gesture of technical superiority, if the Americans should refuse to provide mooring facilities. Unfortunately, in early 1919, the world was not yet officially at peace, only in a state of truce; the Armistice was correctly believed to have ended the war, but the Treaty of Versailles had yet to be signed and the international situation was still strained. Count von Zeppelin had died in 1917 and his successor, Dr. Hugo Eckener, realized how provocative such a demonstration of German prowess would be and advised against it. Nevertheless, preparations went ahead in secret and L.72 was suitably modified. More petrol tanks were installed and extra lift was obtained by the dangerous expedient of preparing to fly without water ballast. Her sister ship, L.71, was similarly prepared by her crew on their own initiative. Unlike their comrades, they planned to fly L.71 across to the United States and then to continue westwards until all the fuel was exhausted. The ship would then be moored or abandoned, having triumphantly proved to the world the viability of the zeppelin for inter-continental travel. Both these gallant attempts proved abortive, for the Inter-Allied Control Commission learned of the projects and insisted on their cancellation.

The third dirigible competitor in 1919 was not generally considered to be in serious contention; she was too small and too primitive. The U.S. Navy blimp C.5, under the command of Lieutenant-Commander Coil, left Long Island on 14 May without arousing any great hopes as to her prospects. Just under twenty six hours later she landed safely in Newfoundland and was there moored and refuelled while her crew rested before embarking on the final stage. All at once, her challenge became credible until, like so many other airships before and since, C.5 fell a victim to unforeseen squalls. A powerful wind suddenly snatched the blimp from her moorings and although the two crew-members still on board were able to jump to safety, the airship herself disappeared without trace into the grey expanse of the North Atlantic.

One other airship awaited her turn: R.34. The motives which impelled the British Government to send their new vessel on her historic flight were strangely confused. The *Daily Mail* prize was, after all, only that newspaper's recognition of a deeper challenge: when men have overcome one obstacle, their thoughts turn always to the next. As soon as the war ended, many of Britain's airmen looked to the possibility of a transatlantic crossing, and the decision of the Admiralty to lend R.34 to the Air Ministry for long-range

Air-Commodore Edward Maitland, C.M.G., D.S.O., A.F.C., 1880 – 1921.
(Royal Aeronautical Society)

flights shows that the project had been discussed previously. Already, tentative proposals for a commercial transatlantic service had been put forward by Armstrong Whitworth, Beardmore and Cunard, subject to a successful demonstration of the airship's capability, and on 4 March a meeting at the Air Ministry had discussed the possibility of such a flight. Then, on 13 March, the President of the Aero Club of America, Alan R. Hawley, despatched a telegram to the Air Ministry, asking Britain to send an airship to a meeting of various aviation groups which was to be held in Atlantic City, New Jersey, the following May. At the time of the request, R.34 had not yet made her trial flight, and Ministry officials alternated between reluctance and eagerness to accept the invitation, which gave expression to the wishes of many Britons. Finally, after considerable discussion, it was decided that R.34 should indeed go.

Stringent conditions were insisted upon, however, particularly with regard to the supply of hydrogen, and these the American Aero Club were unable to meet. By now, in any case, it was evident that the aviation meeting in New Jersey would have come and gone before R.34 was fully ready, but the U.S. Navy stepped in and offered to provide facilities and men for mooring, as well as cylinders of gas and other necessary supplies. Eventually, three reasons were publicly advanced for making the journey. The first two of these, as expected, were to prospect the conditions prevailing in the North Atlantic which might affect future air travel, particularly the meteorological aspect, and to show the capabilities of a rigid airship for long-distance travel. The third, significantly, was to demonstrate the airship in the United States and to 'forge a new link, by way of the air' between the two countries. It is the rather vague terms of this last which make one suspect that the real motives behind the whole exercise were less utilitarian than romantic and patriotic. This suspicion is strengthened when one looks beyond the collective anonymity of the Air Ministry officials at the one man to whose unremitting persuasion and zeal the whole airship programme was indebted.

Air Commodore Edward Maitland, as he ultimately became, was born on 21 February 1880, and was thus thirty nine on the occasion of his finest hour. After taking his degree at Trinity College, Cambridge, he entered the Essex regiment in time to see active service during the Boer War. Afterwards he returned to England and to the monotony of peacetime soldiering — a monotony he alleviated by directing his energies to aviation in all its aspects. Ballooning was an early and abiding interest and one he pursued with enthusiasm. In 1908, along with Professor Gaudron and C. C. Turner, he made an ascent from Crystal Palace in the *Mammoth* balloon of 100,000 cubic ft capacity and covered a record-breaking 1,117 miles before coming down at Mateki Derevni in Russia. Possibly as a result of this exploit he was appointed to the Balloon School at Farnborough and to the Air Battalion a year later. At about this time he turned briefly to aeroplanes and managed both to make and to fly one of his own: an achievement he then capped by selling it to the army as one of the earliest of all British military aircraft. One of his rare accidents was incurred on this aeroplane, when he broke both ankles. At least one of Maitland's friends considered his active career to be at an end and visited the hospital to commiserate with him. "What will you do when you get better?" he enquired solicitously. Maitland shrugged — "Oh, just fly", he answered. And so he did, both professionally and in his leisure hours.

When the growing importance of aircraft was recognized by the formation of the Air Battalion, Major Maitland became commanding officer of No 1 Squadron (Airships). Thereafter, he concentrated his activities on lighter-than-air craft, continually urging his superiors to recognize and rectify the growing superiority of Germany in this field. When the Royal Flying Corps replaced the Air Battalion in 1912, it was divided into an Army Wing and a Naval Wing, of which the latter eventually became the Royal Naval Air Service and passed under the control of the Admiralty. In January 1914, all airships were taken over by the Navy and so Maitland transferred, together with other airship personnel.

The first months of the war saw Wing-Commander Maitland in Belgium, in charge of the non-rigid airship, *Beta,* and some captive balloons intended for artillery spotting. Recognising almost at once that the kite balloons used by the Belgians were superior to their British counterparts, Maitland made drawings and returned to England to recommend a change of design. Not for the last time, his enthusiasm carried its point and before many months had passed, the alterations he proposed had been put into successful effect. The following year, as Wing-Captain, he was appointed commanding officer of the Kite Balloon Station at Roehampton, a pre-war ballooning centre. Here his somewhat eccentric individuality earned him both admiration and affection, for he was never a man to stand upon the dignity of rank or to let someone else take the risks. Kite balloons were not notably stable and occasionally they would break loose or be shot away from their moorings. Maitland felt sure that such a runaway could be landed safely and, to establish the fact beyond dispute, he let slip one which he himself was piloting and landed it without harm.

During the same period, he carried out many experiments, all personal, with parachutes. If his obsession with airships seems misguided nowadays, he was also one of the first men to realize the value of parachutes, and he never ceased to enjoy using them or to recommend their more general adoption. In October 1913, he became the first man to parachute from an airship — the non-rigid *Delta* — and a year or so later he jumped over London from a height of some 11,000 ft. Falling for almost a quarter of an hour before reaching the ground, he became almost unconscious from the cold. His point, however, was assuredly made. Indeed, it was for these and similar exploits that he was subsequently awarded the D.S.O.

A short spell of most uncongenial administrative work at the Admiralty ended in 1916 when he went to take charge of the new airship station at Pulham in Norfolk for a year. Recalled once more to the Admiralty in the summer of 1917, he was appointed Supervisor of Airships and from this position of strength he contrived the increase in Britain's rigid airship programme which was now culminating in R.34. The April of 1918 brought about considerable reorganization of the armed services and although the Admiralty retained control of the airships, the personnel of the Airship Service were transferred to the R.A.F., when Maitland was promoted to the rank of Brigadier-General and the status of Britain's senior airship officer.

General Maitland never married, although he was remembered as a 'great charmer' and his friends claimed to have lost count of the number of young ladies who at one time or another believed themselves engaged to him. He was admired and liked by all his officers, not least because there was a cheerful element of the quixotic about him and a strong disinclination to observe the customary formalities of his position. Still meeting a common reluctance to accept the parachute as a life-saver, he vowed that he would henceforth never leave an airship save by this spectacular means. With only a few exceptions, he kept his promise and the logic of his views was eventually to be accepted. In the meantime, one can be certain that the pleasures of parachuting were enhanced by the satisfaction of an acceptable excuse. When the decision was taken to send R.34 to America, there was no question as to who should be the senior officer on board. Keeping General Maitland at home would have required an Act of Parliament!

Major G. H. Scott, C.B.E., A.F.C., 1888 – 1930. (Central Press)

R.34 being 'walked out' by men and women workers at the Beardmore factory. (Royal Aeronautical Society)

CHAPTER 5

Preparations

H.M.A.R.34 was completed in December 1918 and her lift and trim trials were carried out successfully on the 20th of that month. But because of the persistently bad weather it was not until the following March that she left her hangar at Inchinnan, near Glasgow, where the Beardmore Company had their works. Her new captain was Major George Herbert Scott, a former naval man who had been flying airships since the beginning of the war, when he had commanded H.M. Airship No.4, which frequently escorted the troop transports crossing to France. After three years, he had become captain of No.9 and had even managed a North Sea patrol and a safe night landing with that rather uninspiring dirigible. On the strength of his wide experience, he had been chosen to command R.34 and for a year he had watched her gradually take shape under the hands of the Scottish workers. His wife, Jessie, was the daughter of Beardmore's senior yard manager at Inchinnan and when asked by her friends if she felt anxious about the airship, she replied, 'My father built her and my husband commands her. Why should I worry?' Her faith was shared by all those who had dealings with either the airship or her commander, and it was to be a faith justified by events. Major Scott — known to everyone as 'Scotty' — was no hard disciplinarian and he commanded obedience, respect and affection by his extraordinary and already legendary skill with airships, his unvarying imperturbability and his friendly approach to even the lowliest crew-member. Whatever contingency arose, his men had complete trust in his ability to bring them through in safety.

The Second Officer, Captain Geoffrey Greenland, was a former sailor who had commanded the sloop *Bluebell* before transferring to the R.N.A.S. Shortly after joining the Airship Service he had contracted tuberculosis — a disease often fatal in those days — but in some manner he had avoided either demobilisation or relegation to ground duties. He later made a complete recovery.

On 14 March, R.34 was brought out from her hangar at Inchinnan and her crew began the task of accustoming themselves to their new charge. The factory hands were as proud of their handiwork as were the crew, and several of the girls clubbed together to buy a cloth mascot: a life-size black cat which they fastened to the forward gondola. The maiden flight, lasting nearly five hours, was uneventful and the ship was returned safely to her hangar. On 24 March, despite cold, windy conditions with intermittent fog, snow and hail, R.34 left Inchinnan in the late afternoon for a more extended trial. Although many airship secrets had been wrested from the Germans, none of their manuals of airmanship was as yet available and neither captain nor crew was certain how R.34 would react under differing conditions. All airships were individuals and possessed vices and virtues undetectable in advance of actual experience.

As R.34 was not yet commissioned, Major Scott was accompanied by the Admiralty

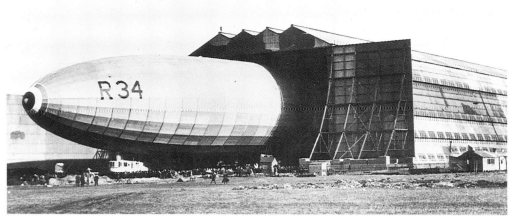

R.34 leaves the hangar of the Beardmore factory at Inchinnan. (Royal Aeronautical Society)

acceptance officer, Colonel William Hicks, who was officially in charge until the ship had been proved. At first, all went well; R.34 lifted easily from the ground and flew with the smooth steadiness that was to be an enduring and endearing characteristic. She went first down the Clyde, then turned to port and flew across the north of England towards Newcastle, before swinging round in a south westerly sweep past Liverpool and over the Irish Sea to Dublin and then back towards the Isle of Man. During the night, the ship appeared to become nose-heavy and ballast was dropped to correct this, but with the coming of daylight, it was discovered that the port elevator had jammed down, so lifting the tail and forcing the airship downwards. The engines were stopped and at once the airship soared steeply upwards. The walking-way was canted to a precarious slope and those using it had to hold tightly to the lifeline positioned above. Others clung on to the girders for support and some of the fuel tanks broke away from their slings in the keel, leaking petrol and tearing through the linen outer cover. They plunged towards the sea below, streaming clouds of petrol vapour behind them, as the airship shot up at accelerated speed, her nose pointing skyward and the gas expanding rapidly. Captain Greenland climbed along the keel corridor to check the fast distending gasbags, at least one of which came near to bursting, but the automatic valves released the pressure and the rate of climb gradually slackened. Finally, at a height of around 8,000 ft, the airship's ceiling was reached and she stopped rising. Spilt petrol flowed down the taut fabric inside the hull, towards the hatch above the after car, but as the engines had been stopped, there was no fire. Apart from the fuel tanks, nothing important had broken loose and the immediate danger was past.

In the control-cabin, as elsewhere, was considerable confusion, with men trying to remain upright on the steeply angled floor. Despite his official seniority and his long experience, Colonel Hicks must have been aware that his detailed knowledge of R.34 did not compare with that of Major Scott. He is said to have turned to the ship's captain and demanded , 'What do I do now Scotty?' Major Scott, calm as always, took charge and his orders soon brought the ship back under control. Ballast was dropped aft, gas valved forward, and all members of the crew not occupied with essential duties or repairs clambered up the keel towards the bows, where their combined weight helped to level the ship. The jammed controls that had started the trouble were the responsibility of Corporal Bob Burgess and he climbed out to free them with a hefty thrust of his foot. Once more, R.34 became manageable and she was swung round and headed back towards Scotland, gradually losing height as Major Scott nursed her carefully along.

Beyond the loss of the fuel tanks, no real damage had been done, but the hazards of the day were by no means over. Thick fog was encountered on the way home and a storm of snow and hail buffeted the airship. Reaching the airfield at midday, the trail rope was dropped into the hands of the inexperienced landing-party, who pulled R.34 down far too forcefully. So bitter was the cold of the upper air, that icicles still clung to the gondolas and much of the water ballast had frozen in the bags and could not be released. Although the two wing engines were reversed, the ship still came surging down to earth much too fast. Standing together in the after car were Leading Aircraftman Fred Browdie and Sergeant William Gent, both unaware at first of anything amiss. Becoming conscious of the increasing rate of descent, Browdie said in surprise, 'I think we're falling, Bill!' He was cut short by a splintering of struts and a wrenching thud which threw both men off their feet as the airship struck the ground. 'Falling?' remarked Gent wryly as he got up, 'I think we've bloody well fell!'

Girders and wires had snapped, the two wing propellers were both broken and the hull and cars were slightly damaged. But no-one was seriously hurt and the various breakages, although extensive, were by no means irreparable. All the same, except for one incident in New York, R.34 was never again to come so close to disaster until her last flight. In retrospect, it seems clear that only this unfortunate accident prevented the airship from being the first aircraft ever across the Atlantic — eastward or westward.

At the Beardmore factory, Major Scott's father-in-law, Mr. Campbell, addressed the hands and asked for their help in repairing the airship as soon as possible. They responded with a will, men and women alike working long hours to put R.34 back into the race again and to ensure that R.33, waiting at Barlow, did not take her sister's place by default. One thing more was done to ensure future success. Many of the airship's crew were former members of the Royal Navy and they possessed all the old-time sailors' traditional belief in good luck and bad luck. Corporal Burgess contrived to remove the black cat mascot from the front of the control-cabin and to burn it secretly and ceremonially — no-one's feelings would be hurt but there would be no more ill fortune!

The repair work took longer than expected but eventually R.34 was ready for service. At about half past six in the evening of 28 May, she left Inchinnan for the last time and set out for East Fortune, the airship base on the Firth of Forth, where she was to be permanently stationed. For this, her third trial and acceptance flight, she once again carried Colonel Hicks, as well as General Maitland and a small tabby kitten which had appeared in the crew's quarters. Instead of reaching East Fortune in a couple of hours, as expected, the airship lost her way in clouds and fog, and drifted out over the North Sea. Turning back to the coast, she eventually found the aerodrome and cruised in the vicinity all night, waiting for daylight. However, in the early morning the visibility was still so bad that her captain preferred not to risk the hazards of a landing. Instead, he took the ship down to Yorkshire and returned to East Fortune only in the afternoon, when a safe landing was made at half past three, despite lingering mist and a stiff breeze. The crew were by this time extremely hungry, for no food had been carried.

But no technical problems had arisen, so R.34 was duly commissioned and preparations for the transatlantic voyage were hurried forward. No official decision had yet been made, but expectation was not confined to the senior officers; rumour and report had conveyed word to everyone concerned.

A fortnight after arriving at her permanent station, R.34 went with R.29 to fly over Edinburgh, Berwick, the Firth of Forth and May Island. This six-hour flight confirmed earlier impressions of the new airship and she was found to be steady, stable and responsive to the controls. Only the engines gave cause for anxiety, as they never, in fact, ceased to do. Lacking sufficient power to provide an adequate reserve, they were often driven beyond their safe limit and performed accordingly. An inevitable result was the strain imposed upon the engineers, who had constantly to be tending their unreliable charges. R.34 had also to test a new and allegedly superior form of D.F.W.T., intended for use on long sea journeys without visible landmarks. Contrary to earlier practice, this involved the ship carrying the equipment and her operators calculating the bearings themselves, by intercepting transmissions from land stations.

Now that Major Scott and the crew were accustomed to handling their ship, the Government decided to send her on a lengthy testing voyage along the German Baltic shores. Besides providing an extended trial of R.34's capabilities, it was apparently considered that the sight of a British rigid airship cruising along their frontiers might help persuade the German Government to sign the Treaty of Versailles, then awaiting final ratification. The former purpose may have been well served, but the latter hope was surely optimistic; pride rather than fear may well have attended the spectacle of a German-designed dirigible being flown by the enemy. Machine-guns were mounted in the forward car and on the two gun-platforms, but no bombs were carried. Leaving East Fortune on the evening of 17 June, R.34 crossed the North Sea and made her way past Heligoland, towards Wilhelmshaven, Holstein, the Kiel Canal, Hamburg and the Baltic. Towards the end of the outward flight, a German aeroplane appeared and apparently stalked the airship for some way. As a precaution, the crew went to action stations and Major Scott signalled to base before turning the airship northwards and setting course for home. R.34 skirted the neutral coasts of Denmark, Norway and Sweden and at one point, from a low altitude, the airmen looked down upon gun batteries trained upward at the intruder. Crossing the North Sea , a strong adverse wind was encountered and for a short while during the night the airship failed to make any headway at all and even passed twice over the same lightship. Largely to blame for this poor performance was the difficulty of synchronising the two engines in the after car, which ran together on a single gearbox. The starboard one ran erratically and finally broke down completely with a seized big end. There was also trouble with the engine clutches, but no other problems marred the flight and the airship landed in the early hours of 20 June, having been in the air around 56 hours.

By now, the Air Ministry had finally taken the decision to send R.34 to the U.S.A., and it was agreed that she would take the 'Great Circle' route of about 3,000 nautical miles from East Fortune through Newfoundland to New York, which would also avoid the possibility of running out of fuel when still far from land. But although Major Scott was as impatient as anyone, he was obliged to report that 1 July was the earliest possible date for departure; sundry modifications and repairs were needed and the engines had to be overhauled. More time was also required by the Air Ministry for their own preparations and these were put in hand without any further delay. Two warships, *Renown* and *Tiger*, were lent by the Admiralty to provide R.34 with forecasts of weather conditions, while a destroyer was posted to the south-west of Ireland to stand by in case of trouble. Should R.34 encounter any difficulties, it was hoped she might reach one of the ships so as to be taken in tow, in which event they were recommended to pull her three points off-wind at a speed of 25 knots. However, these precautions would almost certainly have failed to save the dirigible had she needed assistance, for subsequent events were to prove that sighting particular ships in the vastness of the Atlantic was mostly a matter of luck, wireless communication notwithstanding. Were the voyage to be curtailed at the start, or fuel to run short on the return journey, a reserve landing-party was to stand by at Fermoy, an air station in County Cork. There, R.34 could be sure of skilled help in an emergency landing. Plans were also made for R.34's reception in America. The U.S. Navy had agreed to provide hydrogen, fuel and facilities, but men skilled in the handling of large airships were hard to find, for the Americans at this time had no rigid airships of their own. Accordingly, Lieutenant-Colonel Lucas and Major Fuller, both of the R.A.F., were despatched to the United States with a party of eight experienced airmen, to form the nucleus of an American handling-party.

In the Air Ministry itself, a room was set aside for the venture. Here, wireless messages were to be received or transmitted and some degree of control exercised over the airship, whose position was to be recorded on a wall chart. Although a tentative plan to show the airship's progress on a large illuminated map placed in Trafalgar Square was not implemented, the public would not have to rely on newspapers alone for their information. Marconi House came to the rescue by displaying a chart on which the course was to be regularly plotted from wireless information. Public interest was intense and many reporters arrived at East Fortune in search of information. Some of them were apprehensive about the venture, but the crew were unfailingly optimistic. 'Tiny is a wonderfully strong bus!' Captain Greenland assured one such enquirer. Nothing was left to chance, however, and R.34 was checked throughout, the faulty engine replaced, the bomb racks exchanged for food-lockers and a compass placed on the top gun-platform away from possible electrical interference (no guns were to be carried). Tables and wash-basins were installed in the crew space, which was made five feet longer and furnished with lightweight curtains to keep out draughts. Along the keel an additional twenty-four petrol tanks were fitted, bringing the total fuel capacity up to about 6,000 gallons: sufficient for a more than adequate safety margin.

For this special occasion, the normal wartime complement of twenty-two men was inevitably increased. Two more men were needed to cope with the extra maintenance and flying duties, and meteorological, wireless and navigating officers were required for the specific purposes of the voyage. In courtesy to the U.S. Naval Airship Service, Lieutenant-Commander Zachary Lansdowne was invited as their special representative, and the Admiralty also had their own technical observer aboard in the person of Major J. E. M. Pritchard, who acted as honorary photographer for the voyage. In view of this officer's subsequent fame as the 'Aerial Columbus' of American newspapers, it is interesting to note that his family background fitted him peculiarly well for the first transatlantic flight westwards. Although born and brought up in England, he was American by descent, for his father had left the United States after the defeat of the Confederacy in the Civil War. By another odd genealogical twist, one of his great-great-grandfathers had stepped ashore from the *Sirius,* the first ship to cross the Atlantic by continuous steam-power. Major Pritchard had commanded several small airships during the war and had recently been awarded the O.B.E. Finally, came General Maitland, the senior officer present but not himself captain of the airship.

The crew of R.34:
Back Row: Powell, Gray, Watson, Thirlwall, Mort, Northeast, Heath
Standing: Edwards, Cross, Graham (Wopsie), Scull, Gent, Mays, Ripley, Robinson, Forteath,
Browdie (Punch)
Seated: Shotter, Greenland, Lansdowne, Scott (Judy), Cooke, Harris, Luck
On ground: Smith, Parker, Evenden, Burgess
There is apparently no extant photograph which shows every member of the crew which flew the
Atlantic. Maitland, Pritchard, Durrant and Ballantyne are missing here and Heath was one of those
not finally selected. (Author's collection)

The full complement of thirty men — an Air Force crew with Army style ranks flying in a Naval airship — was as follows:

Major G. H. Scott, A.F.C.	Captain
Captain G. S. Greenland	Second Officer
Second Lieutenant H. F. Luck	Third Officer
Second Lieutenant J. D. Shotter	Engineer Officer
Major G. G. H. Cooke, D.S.C.	Navigator
Major J. E. M. Pritchard, O.B.E.	Special Duties
Lieutenant G. Harris	Meteorological Officer
Second Lieutenant R. F. Durrant	Wireless Officer
Lieutenant-Commander Z. Lansdowne	Representing U.S. Navy
Brigadier-General E. M. Maitland, C.M.G.,D.S.O.	Special Duties
Warrant Officer W. R. Mayes	First Coxswain
Flight-Sergeant W. J. Robinson	Second Coxswain
Sergeant H. M. Watson	Rigger
Corporal R. J. Burgess	Rigger
Corporal F. Smith	Rigger
Leading Aircraftman F. P. Browdie	Rigger

Leading Aircraftman J. Forteath	Rigger
Corporal H. R. Powell	Wireless Telegraphy
Aircraftman 1st Class W. J. Edwards	Wireless Telegraphy
Flight-Sergeant W. R. Gent	Engineer
Flight-Sergeant R. W. Ripley	Engineer
Flight-Sergeant N. A. Scull	Engineer
Sergeant A. G. Evenden	Engineer
Sergeant J. Thirlwall	Engineer
Corporal E. P. Cross	Engineer
Corporal J. H. Gray	Engineer
Leading Aircraftman G. Graham	Engineer
Leading Aircraftman J. S. Mort	Engineer
Aircraftman 2nd Class J. Northeast	Engineer
Aircraftman 2nd Class R. Parker	Engineer

The crew was divided into two watches: port and starboard. In addition to the R.N.A.S. uniforms which they mostly still wore, the crew were issued with heavy-duty flying-suits, incorporating life-saving collars and integral parachute harness. The parachutes themselves were of the 'Guardian Angel' type and were hung in their packs from convenient girders and could be clipped to the suits in a moment. No ripcords were in use at this time and the parachutes were designed to be pulled from their packs by the weight of the wearer jumping clear — if necessary, straight through the linen outer cover of the hull.

Two carrier pigeons also formed part of the establishment, although no-one was very certain what particular purpose their presence served. As General Maitland pointed out later, even if not released, they would be sure of fame as the first of their kind to fly the Atlantic. They came from East Fortune lofts and had been trained to fly home from airships flying over the North Sea. Consequently, there was some speculation as to how they would react in this novel situation. One tentative and rather callous proposal was to liberate them within sight of Ireland on the way home and see whether they would make for land or head in their customary westward direction. For the time being, however, they were safe enough in a wickerwork cage suspended from a keel girder. There had been some talk of taking the captain's Scotch terrier, Judy, as a mascot, but at the last moment she joined the three airmen who were also being left out — in their case to save weight.

Now, on the evening of 1 July, the last preparations and loading neared completion. Three tons of water-ballast (one ton each at bow, amidships and stern), nearly one ton of oil, almost half a ton of drinking water, as well as food, engine spares and many other items, both official and personal, had already been stowed away. Various official letters addressed to American and Canadian dignitaries had also been taken aboard, as well as a small packet of platinum for a privileged New York jeweller. The airship was still firmly anchored and the gasbags filled to their absolute limit, contrary to the normal practice of allowing a small amount of room for expansion. It remained only to fuel the ship and for her to be 'weighed off'. This process involved balancing the weight of petrol against the lift of the hydrogen, so that the maximum amount of fuel would be carried while still leaving sufficient buoyancy for the airship to leave the ground cleanly. Too much lift had also to be avoided, for this would only mean that the weight carried had been restricted unnecessarily. Slowly, in the gloom of the vast hangar, this final operation was finished and R.34 took aboard 4,900 gallons of petrol. Cautiously, she was tested for lift. With only a little less than sixteen tons of fuel in the tanks, the airship just floated. This was less than her theoretical maximum, and no doubt a result of the extra weight of men, equipment, food, drink and spares that she carried. Major Scott would have wished to take on even more fuel if possible, but with petrol forming two-thirds of his entire load he had to be content.

All the disappointments of the past weeks were forgotten in the expectation of adventure. While East Fortune had been in the throes of preparation, Commander Read of the N.C.4 had reached Europe and John Alcock had made his undignified but historic landing in an Irish swamp. R.34 could never now be the first aircraft across the Atlantic, or even the first to make the journey non-stop. But the east-west crossing, the more difficult of the two, was still an unconquered challenge.

R.34 landing at East Fortune. (Fleet Air Arm Museum)

CHAPTER 6

Westward

The official departure time had been fixed for 2 a.m. Greenwich Mean Time (3 a.m. British Summer Time) on the morning of Wednesday, 2 July, in order to obtain the most lift possible. At midnight the crew sat down to a hearty supper and drank the health of R.34 before leaving to don their heavy flying suits and take their places in the airship, fastened down and ready in her floodlit hangar. When the final preparations had been completed, the handling-party grouped themselves around the grey bulk. There were nearly seven hundred of them all told: airmen, members of the women's branch and soldiers of the Black Watch. Together they took hold of ropes, rails and guys, releasing the airship from her moorings and holding her down by their own strength and weight. A tractor laboriously pulled aside the heavy sliding door and as Major Scott gave the order, 'Walk her out!' the bugler took up the command. Guided and carried by the swarm of handlers about her, R.34 emerged from the hangar very slowly, like a moth from its chrysalis. Overhead, low clouds and mist obscured the sky and a slight wind from the north-east brought flurries of rain to increase the biting cold. The weather forecast for the Atlantic had been favourable, however, and Major Scott had decided to wait no longer. Gradually and carefully, the airship was swung round to point into the wind and there she paused on the brink of flight as the last adjustments were made. As the engine telegraph rang out, the engines coughed and spluttered reluctantly into life, spinning slowly for two or three minutes to warm up. In the control-cabin, Major Scott waited with General Maitland until word was received from Lieutenant Shotter that all was ready. With the captain was Sergeant Murray Watson, acting as steering coxswain, and Warrant Officer Walter Mayes, who stood facing right and sideways to the line of flight, his eyes watching the inclinometer and his hands grasping the elevator wheel. Of the two, it was he who had the more skilled task, for a good elevator coxswain was supposed to sense the trim of the ship with his feet, besides watching the instruments and obeying instructions. Mayes' ability was already a byword and it was claimed that crew-members in the far corners of the ship could deduce his presence at the wheel from the steadiness of R.34's flight.

Crowded into the cabin behind these four were the navigation officer and others whose duties lay in the ship's nerve centre. To one side, in full view of everyone, there hung the large dial of the altimeter, positioned so that its vital information could never be overlooked.

It was now eighteen minutes ahead of schedule — 1.42 a.m. G.M.T. — and as Major Scott signalled, 'Let go all!', the sharp notes of the bugle shrilled out above the sound of the engines. Immediately, the handling-party released the guys and R.34, freed from all external weight, lifted ponderously into the overcast sky. Again the engine telegraph sounded and with clutches engaged the propellers spun to the heightened roar of the

Major G. G. H. Cooke, D.S.C., on the left, and Lieutenant J. D. Shotter at the open window of the forward car. (Author's collection)

engines. Gathering momentum and rising slowly, the airship was soon lost to view in the engulfing clouds. Even as she circled to set her course north-west for the Clyde, there came faintly to the ears of the crew the sound of a thousand voices, joined together in a farewell burst of cheering. Dropping a quarter of the main water-ballast and so leaving only a meagre three quarters of a ton amidships for future use, Major Scott took the airship up higher and increased the engine revolutions to 1600. The telegraph rang out a signal to the four engine rooms and the power deployed showed on the dials to his left. Everyone on board knew that the start of a long airship voyage was potentially the most hazardous part. Each minute brought its small consumption of petrol and its tiny decrease in overall weight, so the further a ship travelled, the lighter she became and the higher she could safely ascend. In order to carry the greatest possible weight of fuel, the captain had filled R.34 to her maximum capacity, with both petrol and hydrogen. At nearly ground level, her static lift had been only just sufficient to raise her clear of the immediate obstacles and even the release of ballast had not taken her much higher. Once in the air, the power of the engines had thrust her forwards and provided the dynamic lift that raised her further and was now keeping her aloft, for she was soon flying about a ton heavy. Ahead of her, invisible in the darkness, were the Scottish hills, so the next hour would be critical, with the ship being in danger if flown either too high or too low. If she were to force her way upwards, the decreased air pressure would cause even more of the hydrogen in the already taut gasbags to expand and leak away through the automatic valves and until the fuel supply burnt lower, this further loss of lift would pose a threat to safety. At first there was no need for the choice, as the course plotted by Major Cooke led along the Firth of Forth and no great height was required. By now, the first clouds had cleared, and from their gondola windows, the airmen stared down 1,300 ft to the lights of Rosyth and a plume of white smoke streaming from the red glow of a passing express train. Although most of the actual Atlantic crossing was to be in the teeth of the prevailing winds, at this stage of the journey there was a following breeze of 25 m.p.h., sweeping R.34 forward at a ground-speed of 65 m.p.h. In the wireless room directly behind the control-cabin Lieutenant Durrant and his men were bent over the W.T. equipment, transmitting, receiving or scribbling as the routine and congratulatory messages flowed to and fro.

After the airship left the Firth of Forth, the hazards threatening her did not materialise; she flew to the south of the Lennox Hills of Stirlingshire, managing to keep at a fairly low altitude but also to avoid the higher ground. Glasgow eventually came into sight on the port beam and R.34, passing over her birthplace as the light increased, moved onwards down the Clyde, where strong winds from the Dumbarton hills buffeted and tossed her. In the control-cabin, Major Scott and General Maitland watched the mercury of the inclinometer disappear momentarily as the airship tilted up twenty four degrees at the bow and pitched back and forth with surprisingly gradual movement. Lieutenant Harris, the meteorological officer, was certain that this air disturbance could be avoided by rising above 6,000 ft, but his advice had to be ignored, as he must have expected. Keeping R.34 below 1,500 ft, Major Scott piloted her steadily onwards as the conditions slowly improved. Changing from grey to pink behind the airship, the dawn sky showed a solitary steamship on the sea below, whose crew waved a greeting to the airmen.

By now the seven men crowded into the control-cabin were feeling the strain after a long and busy night without sleep. Even General Maitland dozed uncomfortably on a fresh-water tank for some minutes before giving up the attempt and moving off to his hammock. There were only fifteen of these, slung on both sides of the keel from the side girders and shared by the two watches, turn and turn about. He was not accustomed to this way of sleeping, for senior officers were usually allocated something distinctly better, but with a little assistance, he clambered in. Sleeping soundly, if briefly, he rolled out in time to join the watch coming on at breakfast, but took care not to put his feet on the thin fabric of the ship's outer cover as he did so. While he had been asleep, Rathlin Island had been passed at 4.39 a.m. G.M.T. and ahead of the airship lay more than two thousand miles of open sea. Conditions had changed rapidly and the earlier clear skies had given way to thick, rolling mist into which R.34, still at a low altitude, had become gradually buried.

The first sunlight had briefly caused a rise in the temperature of the gas which had caused it to expand and escape through the automatic release valves. This form of loss could not occur in a lightly loaded ship with gasbags not fully inflated, but in one heavily laden and already with maximum gas pressure, there was little margin of safety. Now that heavy mist and rain surrounded the ship, the gas had contracted again and the consequent loss of lift was further accentuated by moisture clinging to the outer cover. Although to some extent the effect was countered by the weight of fuel consumed, as yet this was slight. Major Scott sought to escape beneath the clouds, but they were too low and he was obliged to bring R.34 back up through the enveloping vapour, flying her at an angle of as much as twelve degrees in order to keep aloft. In its turn, this spoiled the aerodynamic lines she presented when horizontal, so the speed and petrol consumption both suffered in consequence. Aggravating these handicaps was the need to rest the engines periodically; they were already proving troublesome and the one in the forward car had been shut down since six o'clock. The starboard engine in the after car was new and had only recently been fitted in place of that which had caused difficulties during the Baltic flight. It was now running under load for the first time, for the engineers had completed its installation only a few hours before the flight began. Indeed, as R.34 had made her way down the Clyde, they had still been cleaning up the gondola and throwing overboard bits of wire, bolts and other discarded oddments.

At breakfast the officers, all enthusiasts, discussed the technical problems they were encountering and agreed that the pitching so far endured was much less than would be suffered by seaborne travellers — their theory receiving considerable support from the circumstance that no one showed any sign of airsickness. Before the voyage reached its end, tempers were to become somewhat strained with the tensions of dangerous work and prolonged discomfort. Fortunately, there were few opportunities for disagreement, as most of the crew passed their working hours in lonely isolation and only at mealtimes were they brought together. The sole point of dissension that had arisen so far, more humorous than serious, concerned the mysterious appropriation of Captain Greenland's toothbrush to mix the mustard. Despite overcrowding in the living quarters, the age-old segregation of officers and men was still strictly preserved. On the far side of the dividing curtain, the other ranks ate their meal to the sound of jazz records played on a rather tinny gramophone and helping to keep any disrespectful comments from the ears of their nearby superiors. Both watches, men and officers alike, had now settled down to the routine of regular tasks, regular rest and regular sleep, for the restricted working, living and sleeping quarters permitted little flexibility.

By nine o'clock the layer of fog in which they were now travelling had sunk a little and R.34, at an altitude of 1,500 ft, found herself sailing above an enormous sea of clouds, stretching to the horizon in all directions. Around was clear air but more than 6,000 ft above, another cloud layer covered the sky and obscured the sun. Between the two grey wildernesses, in a featureless world of her own, the airship flew without sight of sky or sea and with only the tumbled cloud masses passing under her keel to show that she moved. Some meteorological twist had given R.34 a charge of static electricity and there was slight discharge from the ship to the clouds. The wireless operators reported that the shocks were fairly serious but no one on board was unduly concerned. All the crew were accustomed to this effect and accepted it as an almost inevitable and usually harmless phenomenon. When an airship's trail rope struck the ground at the end of a flight it sometimes earthed any such charge of electricity. In R.34, all parts of the metal framework were earthed to the engines in order that the exhaust gases would act as a conductor to reduce the danger from sparks or lightning. The chance of conflagration was remote and could be virtually ignored; most crew-members tended to worry more about the possibility of fire from petrol.

Before very long, the clouds above the airship began to clear and through widening gaps the sun shone down, drying the outer cover and once again threatening to heat the gas. As the ship was still heavy and the gasbags still full, Major Scott was anxious to conserve all the hydrogen he could, and this time he possessed the means of avoiding the sunlight's full effect. Skilful handling of the elevator wheel brought R.34 down into the mist below, so that the cold dampness protected her hull from the direct sunshine. The measure of the coxswain's accuracy was shown when Major Cooke climbed the long ladder from the keel to the gun-platform at the top of the hull. Here, nearly a hundred feet above the control-cabin, he stood to take a fix on the sun with his sextant. For lack of a visible ocean horizon, he used the distant cloud horizon and obtained a roughly accurate position without difficulty. He was amused to find that although the airship was covered, the mist ended abruptly at his shoulders, leaving his upper body out in the open. An independent observer, had there been one, would have been puzzled to account for the disembodied head skimming over the clouds, "like St John the Baptist's on a plate", as the navigator described it later.

Inside the airship it was cold and damp, the moisture dripping off fabric and girders as the ship ploughed doggedly on through the wet fog. The two engines in the after car were now rested for a while, and that in the forward gondola took over the drive. A slight east wind was still blowing R.34 on her way, contrary to expectations, and at eleven o'clock Major Scott decided to economise on his fuel by cutting out this engine also, and using the two in the wing cars only. This gave the ship an airspeed of some 35 m.p.h., but a correspondingly lower petrol consumption. As the wind-assisted ground-speed was still in excess of 40 m.p.h., it was probably a wise compromise.

If the engineers were busy, so were the riggers, who attended to a multiplicity of jobs, including that of inspecting and — if necessary — repairing the gasbags with patches and

Somewhere above the Atlantic. The elevator coxswain is in the centre and the steering coxswain on the left. (Author's collection)

rubber solution. This job was not without its own peculiar hazards and it was not unknown for a man to fall right through the thin cotton fabric and into the gas. Although this never happened in R.34, the possibility was always present and some of the riggers carried knives in their belts to cut themselves free before they should be overcome by suffocation. They usually sang or whistled while at work, for if the notes sounded higher, it was an indication and warning of leaking gas. Like the topmen of the old-time sailing ships, they were also accustomed to going aloft in conditions that would have terrified most landsmen. Periodically, someone had to clamber up the long ladder to the top of the hull and make his way nearly two hundred yards to the stern gun-pit, abaft the tail fins, inspecting the outer cover and gas outlets as he did so. Entirely in the open and swept by the full force of the airstream, the top girder was furnished only with a single rope which could be grasped by anyone nervous enough to require reassurance. Long service in airships over the boisterous North Sea had accustomed most of the riggers to such dangerous routines and they usually walked upright, disdaining any assistance, even when the airship was tilted steeply. For a man walking towards the bows of the ship, it was necessary to lean slightly forwards, against the rush of air. When walking aft, a backward lean was similarly needed. Apart from such maintenance, there were many minor tasks which fell to their lot. Plenty of heat was available from the starboard engine exhaust-pipe and before long, one of the riggers was seated over a basin in his shirt sleeves, peeling potatoes. It was hardly an adventurous occupation, but his mates probably assured him that it was an historic one, since nobody had ever peeled potatoes over the Atlantic before.

The ship was now about four hundred miles from East Fortune, way out over the Atlantic, and when the next landfall came it would be the North American continent, two thousand miles ahead through the swirling and still thickening clouds. The watches alternated spells of duty and had their meals in two sittings — the men coming on having their meal half an hour before those going off. With nothing to see through the windows, the beef stew and potatoes of lunch provided a welcome break for everyone, as well as revealing a minor design fault in R.34. The living and dining quarters were situated some way forward of the centre of gravity, and when fifteen men assembled there for meals, their combined weight caused the ship's nose to drop appreciably. Various members of the lower ranks had perforce to take their food aft and eat it squatting on the walking-way at the greatest possible distance from the bows. Care had to be exercised when moving along the keel, for the walking-way was now becoming slippery in places, where oil had been left by the engineers' boots. Half a dozen times during the voyage men slipped and were in some danger of falling right through the outer cover.

Hazard, as well as inconvenience, was inevitably attendant upon R.34's cooking facilities. On one occasion, as the duty cook was handed a saucepan of boiling water from the engine-car, the lid was forced off by the rush of the airstream. It was dashed straight into the propeller, flung against the outer cover and thrown off into the void. When the engine was stopped, the propeller showed signs of damage and in order to find out how serious this was, Lieutenant Shotter, not without trepidation, fastened a rope around his waist and climbed out of the car. He then inched his way backwards until he was able to see that only the canvas covering of the propeller was torn; the wood remained intact and the engine could be run without danger. Nor was this the only incident to disturb the Engineer Officer's peace of mind. Before the flight began, he had prepared for all possible contingencies, even the least likely. It was as well that he did so, for at one point he was called in haste to the port car, where he found Sergeant Ripley pointing to a magneto that had actually caught fire. The flames had been immediately extinguished but the magneto itself was beyond repair and it had to be replaced with a new one which Shotter, against orders to restrict the weight of spares, had fortunately included in his supply.

Like the engineers, the W.T. operators were almost continuously at work and the flow of information went to and fro over the air. They were still in touch with East Fortune and picking up many other signals from a variety of sources. However, the new method of fixing the ship's position by means of wireless bearings had already proved a disappointment. Only one fix had been taken from Clifden on the Irish coast and when the operators there were not transmitting, then nothing could be done, for the periodic acknowledgement signals that were used while receiving were too brief to be of practical use to the airship. There was to be no subsequent improvement in effectiveness and the navigation of R.34 across the Atlantic owed little or nothing to wireless telegraphy.

After lunch, the clouds below the airship began to thin out, while here and there patches of blue sea could again be glimpsed. Major Cooke, using the Beck bombsights, was able to watch the white tips of waves and to compare the course steered with the actual course thus observed. With a northerly wind now blowing, he calculated the southward drift to be 21 degrees, rather more than he had hitherto estimated, and corrections to the course were made accordingly. Such regular checks were necessary if R.34 was not to travel many miles out of her way.

For those in the forward car the tedium of the early afternoon was relieved by a rare visit from the Engineer Officer, who came in eating chocolate and amiably 'dispensing sarcasms', as Harold Luck recorded. Revenge was suitably taken by the theft of his chocolate and he retired to his engines in discomfiture.

Not long before two o'clock, Sergeant Watson brought a dishevelled and pale-faced figure to Major Scott, who stared in astonishment at the totally unexpected addition to his crew. He recognised the stowaway, for such the man was, as Aircraftman William Ballantyne, one of the three crew members who had been excluded at the last minute to make room for more important passengers. Determined not to miss the chance of a lifetime, Ballantyne had told his friends of his intention and for some time now they had been wondering when he would show himself. Major Scott wakened General Maitland and together they interviewed the young airman. There was, in point of fact, very little that could be done about the situation. The General fully appreciated Ballantyne's motives, even if he was obliged to condemn his actions, and he could not conceal a smile as he listened to the young man's story.

Sneaking aboard two hours before lift-off, the stowaway had first hidden himself on top of one of the girders between two of the gasbags. He had originally intended to stay in hiding until America was reached, and he had endured the cold and discomfort until violent sickness had been added to his other sufferings. For as the gasbags tautened, he had been unable to avoid breathing in the hydrogen which had leaked all around him from the release valves. Odourless and tasteless, its insidious effect was nonetheless extremely unpleasant and Ballantyne had been driven out to hide in the keel, where he was soon discovered. By good fortune, he had timed his emergence nicely and the airship was now far from land. Had he come out of hiding earlier, General Maitland would have sent him over the side with a parachute, but the time for that had passed and the airman remained on board until the end of the voyage. The question of punishment had also, of necessity, to be deferred indefinitely. In the meantime, Major Scott could only reflect that even one extra passenger meant an added strain on the ship's resources, as well as having already deprived her of a valuable hundredweight or so of fuel. Ballantyne himself was unrepentant and he was later to declare that having achieved his object, he was quite willing to accept the consequences. For some time yet he was quite ill and after being doctored with quinine by Lieutenant Luck, he rested in one of the hammocks, possibly that vacated by General Maitland. The General himself often slept under the table — a favourite place for all the officers — so he would not have been incommoded by his sacrifice. After a few hours, Ballantyne recovered sufficiently to work his passage for the rest of the journey, mainly by acting as cook or by pumping petrol to the engines.

Very soon, the time came to rest the wing engines, and the other three took over, driving R.34 at a slightly increased airspeed of 40 m.p.h. All through the long afternoon she toiled onwards through thinning clouds which rolled aside ever more frequently to reveal the blue Atlantic a bare 900 ft beneath her keel. The improving weather brought in its train some bizarre effects. At one moment, rainbows ringed both the ship herself and the attendant shadow racing over the water below.

Lieutenant Durrant, the Wireless Officer, was able to report that he was now receiving signals from St. John's, Newfoundland. Still faint, they would increase in strength as the communication with East Fortune and Clifden faded into silence. Contact had also been made with a wireless station in the Azores, so with the goodwill messages that came in periodically from passing ships, there was no dearth of employment for the two wireless operators. Teatime brought the expected bread, butter and jam, served on aluminium plates, and also steaming hot cups of tea brewed over the engine exhaust pipe. Returning afterwards to the control-cabin, General Maitland discovered a second stowaway lurking in the keel. He, or maybe she, was happily of less account than the first and was recognised by the General as the same tabby cat which had accompanied R.34 on her acceptance flight. There was no coincidence to account for Wopsie's presence and although Maitland forbore to enquire closely, subsequent events were to reveal the oldest man on board, forty-two year old Leading Aircraftman George Graham, as the proud owner. He had first found his pet as a stray in Renfrew and she had since become a regular, if unofficial, member of the crew.

The improvement in downward visibility was transitory, and before long the clouds came rolling over and about the ship again, surrounding her with dense, damp fog. Regular wireless reports from *H.M.S. Renown* and *H.M.S. Tiger* showed thick mist or, at best, poor visibility lying ahead, but no gales or strong winds. Major Scott, still nursing his engines, kept all five running at half speed and now judged it safe to increase height, first to 1,200 and then to 2,000 ft. At this safe altitude, the ocean of clouds was left far below: a fleecy white blanket looking very different from the clammy greyness it presented at close quarters. The sky above was a deep and beautiful blue, clear of all cloud traces save high in the south west, where the pale outlines of unusual cirrus forms could just be discerned. Lieutenant Harris recognised them at once for what they were: harbingers of a depression moving northwards to intercept the airship. In the northern hemisphere, the winds of a depression invariably blow anti-clockwise, a vessel on the northern perimeter being driven westwards by their force. Major Scott knew of this effect and prepared to turn it to advantage, by steering his ship across the path of the depression, that its winds might hasten her along. In this, as in other ways, his position was analogous not to that of a modern airline pilot, but rather to that of an old-time man-of-war skipper (with his admiral aboard). Throughout the voyage his concern was not only with harnessing or withstanding the vagaries of wind and weather; he had also to be constantly balancing static and dynamic lift against diminishing weight to produce level flight. Too slow to ignore adverse conditions and too heavily laden to rise above them, R.34 required the guidance of a more than capable hand. All airship voyages conformed to a similar pattern: a problem in three-dimensional control which needed wide and varied skills to master.

At twenty to seven that evening, the clock was put back for the second time, in preparation for the eventual change to New York local time, and not long afterwards a message from the Air Ministry drew a smug look from Lieutenant Guy Harris. It foretold a depression coming up from the south and so provided flattering confirmation of his earlier prediction. With evening came the expected fall in temperature, chilling men and airship alike. Although the ship was now flying at 3,000 ft, the cloud layer had once again risen to her level, so that she plunged in and out of the uneven mist; one moment shrouded in fog, the next back again in the slanting rays of the setting sun. The drop in temperature soon brought about supercooling of the gas and the ship had again to be flown at a pronounced angle to avoid losing height. All five engines drove her forward at nearly full power: an uneconomical arrangement which could have been safely avoided only by dumping fuel as ballast and so producing the same end-result. Under these conditions, R.34's performance was inevitably very unsatisfactory and Major Scott decided to try flying below the clouds. With all the windows shut, the ship descended 1,500 ft through the cold darkness to a low height at which only thin and sporadic mist patches obscured the sea, while above and below the ship the dying sun cast a delusive pink warmth on to the freezing fog banks.

During the evening there came further trouble with the engines, when that in the forward car had to be stopped for three quarters of an hour to repair an oil pipe. But as night fell, Major Scott and his navigator, Major Gilbert Cooke, contemplated the fuel position with satisfaction. Petrol consumption had averaged just over one gallon for each mile covered, and if this low consumption continued, they would reach New York with more than a thousand gallons in hand.

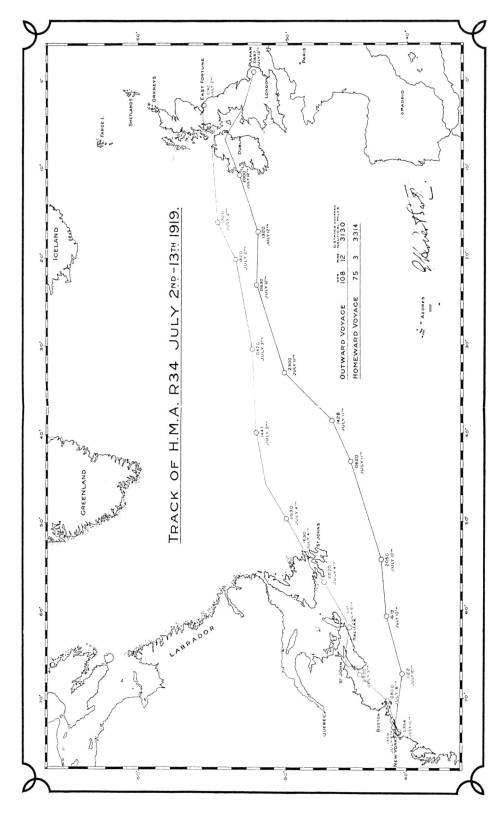

Flight plan of the Atlantic crossings. (Author's collection)

CHAPTER 7

Hazards Overcome

Alcohol was not normally issued to airship crews, as Bovril, Horlicks, cocoa and tea were officially preferred to brandy or the traditional rum by the Air Ministry's Medical Administrator. It was a ruling frequently cursed but rarely more vehemently than by the engineer members of R.34's crew, already deprived of their usual cigarettes. There were eleven of them, working under the command of Lieutenant John Shotter, and of these Sergeant Gent was responsible only for the supply of petrol, which had to be pumped manually to the tanks above the engine cars. On each watch there was thus only one man to each of the deafening, unreliable and temperamental engines: a four-hour shift both arduous and destructive of future sleep.

By twenty past nine the next morning, when the clock was put back once more, R.34 was nearly half way across the Atlantic, out of touch with East Fortune and a hopeful twenty-four hours away from Newfoundland. The wind increased steadily in strength as Lieutenant Harris's expected depression drew nearer but the assistance it eventually provided proved to be disappointingly brief. Before long the winds became both strong and adverse, slowing the airship's progress considerably. Lieutenant Harris had followed up his prediction of the depression with the pessimistic assertion that the western Atlantic invariably harboured fogs or gales: equally ominous prospects for any airship flight. For the present, however, conditions were little different from those of the previous day, with scattered cloud and mist. Later on, the sky cleared and it became possible to see fifty miles in every direction. At about this time R.34 crossed the main steamship routes, east and west. As was to happen so often during the voyage, it was possible to exchange messages with ocean-going vessels, but quite impossible actually to catch sight of them in the vast emptiness of the sea. Wireless contact was also made, for the first time, with the station at Glace Bay in North America.

It now became a matter of some concern to obtain an accurate measurement of the ship's altitude. The aneroid barometer showed it to be 1,200 ft, but this figure was based on a sea-level pressure similar to that at East Fortune, and it was more than likely there would be a difference. An attempt to check this by lowering a sea-level aneroid on a long line was unsuccessful, for the inevitable jolting disturbed the reading before it could be pulled back into the control-cabin. Major Scott finally took advantage of the improved visibility and solved the problem by using a sextant to measure the angle subtended by the ship's shadow. Knowing the length of this, he was able to calculate the height as 2,100 ft, revealing an aneroid error of 900 ft. This estimate was soon confirmed when the nearby *S.S. Canada,* heard but not seen, was able to wireless the reading of her own sea-level barometer to R.34. Another of the captain's brilliantly effective improvisations was also employed during the better visibility. Whenever the ship's shadow passed some clearly defined spot, such as the foam of a breaking wave, its passage was carefully timed by stopwatch and the surface-speed thereby calculated. Around midday the best weather of the entire voyage was experienced, the deep blue of the sea being matched by the light blue of the clear sky overhead, and the overnight chill was forgotten as the crew made the most of the unaccustomed warmth.Some of those off watch relaxed in the fresh air of the gun-pit at the stern of the ship, or even sat on top of the hull nearby, with their backs braced against the upright tail fin.

Anxiety about the engines was general, despite the frequency with which they were rested and the large stock of spares stored in the keel. At two o'clock in the afternoon the starboard wing engine had to be stopped for repairs when it transpired that a leak in the water-jacket had caused a slight loss of coolant. When the various compounds in the tool-kit proved ineffective, Lieutenant Shotter commandeered what was left of the chewing-gum supplied as a smoking substitute. With the enthusiastic help of two engineers, it was quickly masticated and spread on the affected part. A small piece of copper sheeting and a length of adhesive tape completed the repair. A further problem was caused by the failure of three of the manually-operated pumps that were used to transfer petrol to the main tanks. These could not be repaired and only one was left in use.

Towards the end of the afternoon, the strong headwinds backed somewhat and R.34 was carried slightly off-course, pushed northwards in the direction of the distant Greenland coasts. Coming up from the south-south-east and blowing at speeds approaching 50 m.p.h., the gale compelled the airship to fight her way forwards with a sideways motion and brought back the thick, clinging fog and bitter cold which had been escaped for so short an interval. Resuming the full dress they had briefly abandoned during the halcyon afternoon, the crew again donned their flying suits against the chill that could not be kept out even by the silk underclothing supplied specially for the voyage. Fierce gusts and heavy rain struck the ship: a constant, roaring barrage over which the men in the control-cabin shouted their conversation. Water seeped through in many places, soaking charts and weighing heavily upon the already sodden fabric of the hull. Now and again, as the strands of fog thinned and parted for a moment, white-capped waves could be discerned, racing madly across a boiling sea. The ship herself remained surprisingly steady: far more so, in Major Scott's opinion, than her predecessors would have done under similar buffeting. A slow and steady pitching was the only result of this harsh treatment: awkward for fragile movables but without effect on the crew's comfort or stomachs. Now that the weight of petrol had been considerably reduced, Major Scott decided to escape from the gale by climbing above it. As the elevator coxswain spun his wheel, the tail dropped and R.34 moved gradually upwards, cleaving slowly through the murk and reaching the quiet of the upper atmosphere. An hour later, a height of 3,400 ft found her safe above the clouds, riding smoothly, and careless of the storm which still howled below. The cold of the ensuing night brought about no significant loss of buoyancy, for so much petrol had now been consumed that there was an adequate reserve of lift. Through the hours of darkness R.34 droned steadily along: an underpowered craft accomplishing her task by dogged endurance. Alcock and Brown, in a Vickers Vimy, had taken only 16 hours for their crossing, whereas the airship had already been airborne three times as long and was still not in sight of the American continent.

One unexpected phenomenon was already puzzling some of the officers: each night, as the ship duly became heavier, the tail became even more so, causing the airship to assume a nose-up attitude. So marked was this effect that although the angle provided necessary dynamic lift, it was too strong and had to be reduced by putting the elevators slightly down. In the mornings the opposite happened and for a time the elevators had to be put up. This odd behaviour persisted throughout both parts of the voyage and was the subject of much speculation. Meanwhile, most members of the crew were too immersed in their own problems or too sleepy to worry.

Lieutenant Shotter, especially, was very tired; his men might also be hardworked and sleepless, but as Engineer Officer he alone had to carry the full weight of responsibility for the engines. Their unsatisfactory design and performance made his job no sinecure and he spent his time clambering from one engine-room to another, mostly unaware of what was happening elsewhere. Fortunately, he was a placid man and accustomed to going many hours without sleep. His wife was waiting for him in Scotland and round his neck he wore a pair of her silk stockings as a combination of muffler and lucky charm against mishap. His job on the airship was vital but its tedium acceptable, for any excitement must have been produced only by a danger or hazard he could well do without. Shortly after midnight he opened the window of one of the engine cars for a breath of outside air and was understandably surprised to see faintly through the gloom another airship car, flying a few yards away on a parallel course. From its open window an engineer was looking straight across at him. Before his surprise could become vocal, he realised that he was seeing only himself: an uncanny reflection outlined against a bank of thick mist.

Early morning brought clearer skies and disclosed a new sight to the men in the control-cabin: the first object they had seen on the water since leaving Ireland astern. The iceberg was about 150 ft high, a dazzling white against the green water which lapped at the base of its towering cliffs. From the air it was also possible to see what were invisible from ocean-level: sharp, angular roots spreading out insidiously to menace unwary shipping. Other icebergs could be seen in the dim distance, few at first but increasing in numbers until the ocean was dotted with small, broken pack ice.

As the morning wore on, the gas warmed to the sun's heat and Major Scott drove the airship down again into the clouds which had collected into their usual low-lying pattern of sporadic denseness. Newfoundland was not far ahead and its approach was soon heralded by more swirling fog, closing on the ship in a stranglehold of grey darkness. Messages were being received from the United States by now, usually consisting of somewhat premature congratulations on R.34's incomplete achievement. These were pinned up on the notice-board in the living quarters: an inadequate surface soon overcrowded with slips of paper. Major Scott's optimism was guarded, however, for the fuel situation had worsened considerably. There were no gauges on the slip tanks, but prolonged use of the dipstick revealed that only 2,200 gallons were left. With strong headwinds to be expected down the coast, this was discouraging news: R.34 would reach America without a doubt but the possibility of getting to New York without stopping was becoming hourly less likely.

Before midday the air suddenly became very cold, when the ship flew over the Labrador current from the Arctic, carrying along great quantities of loose ice. As the ship's gas was still warm, the effect of this contrast was to cause extreme superheating, and had the airship been flying lower, the difference would have been even greater. No threat was presented to R.34 but Major Scott was loth either to hold her down forcibly or to valve gas unnecessarily, so he allowed the airship to ascend once more into the warmer air 4,000 ft above the ice-fields. This was then the ship's pressure height: the altitude at which the gasbags became fully distended and above which the hydrogen would be needlessly lost, so here, for a short while, R.34 maintained a level course. From this vantage point, at ten minutes to one o'clock, local time, Major Scott was, appropriately, the first person to sight land. Through a rare gap in the fog clouds he caught a passing glimpse of small islands: the outposts of America lying off the north coast of Newfoundland. In the control-cabin there was wild excitement for some minutes, with everyone talking at once as the realisation of their success spread quickly through the ship.

Forty minutes later, at 4.30 p.m. G.M.T. and very nearly sixty hours after passing the lighthouse at Rathlin Island, the American continent was reached at Trinity Bay. Not long afterwards the fog thinned again, grew faint and then cleared momentarily from R.34's path to reveal the barren wastes of Newfoundland spread out beneath her keel: bleak lakes, dark forests and empty wilderness where no sign of man's presence could be seen except the great airship herself. The loneliness was in marked contrast to the conditions experienced by the men who were now passing overhead. Crammed together in the restricted living quarters of the airship, there was no privacy for anyone when off watch and very few normal amenities. Most of the men were not only unshaven, but also distinctly dirty, for the supply of fresh water was by now very much depleted. Lieutenant Luck, indulging himself with a rare wash, speculated grimly on the number of men using the same basinful of water — before him as well as after.

Towards the end of the afternoon, after flying through yet more fog patches, R.34 passed over Fortune Bay, where the crew had their first sight of fellow human beings since the sailors of the Clyde steamer had been left behind. Wireless messages were exchanged with St. John's and with New York. From the latter came a question from Lieutenant-Colonel Lucas, in charge of the ground crew, asking when the airship expected to reach Mineola, Long Island, the airfield where his men waited. With a thousand still to be covered, Major Scott replied briefly but hopefully, 'Early Sunday morning.' Various letters, one of them to the Governor, were dropped by parachute before Newfoundland was left astern. The parachute itself failed to open, but the letters were picked up undamaged and subsequently arrived safely at their destinations. Another communication was similarly posted by one of R.34's crew: a picture-postcard of the airship bearing a few words to his wife in Scotland. He dropped it overboard and watched it flutter down towards empty woodland without any serious expectation of having it delivered. Three months later it duly reached his home by a devious and unknown route, only slightly disfigured by souvenir hunters who had snipped off small pieces.

Not far to the south of Newfoundland were the two tiny islets of St. Pierre and Miquelon, proudly flying the tricolour as the only territories in North America still to retain their allegiance to France, two centuries after General Wolfe. With impeccable Gallic chivalry, the French signaller at St. Pierre dipped his flag in salute to the airship as she passed over him. If he expected any acknowledgement, however, he was disappointed. It was hardly worthwhile sending someone down the walking-way to the far stern, for by the time he had reached the White Ensign, the ship would have been two miles or more on her way.

Soon, Nova Scotia came into view and also the tramp steamer S.S. Seal: the first ship to be sighted by the crew since leaving Scotland. The evening was an anxious time, despite clear weather. While his engineers snatched a few minutes' leisure to play pitch and toss with spare washers, Lieutenant Shotter worried over the small amount of fuel still left to his engines. Together with General Maitland and the senior officers, he joined Major Scott in a hurried conference to discuss whether it would still be feasible to reach New York directly, or whether an intermediate stop would be necessary. Major Scott listened attentively, but even General Maitland's presence did not absolve him from the ultimate responsibility and it was he alone who decided that the ship would have to call in at Montauk, on the eastern tip of Long Island, where she could refuel before finishing her journey. It was a reluctant decision, but to take the other course and risk running out of petrol on that final stage would be to court unnecessary danger. The word was passed on accordingly and the American authorities informed of the change of plan.

Among the various aircraft which had earlier assembled for the transatlantic crossing was a Handley-Page aeroplane piloted by Major Brackley and Rear-Admiral Mark Kerr. Disappointed of their chance to win the *Daily Mail* prize and hampered by technical troubles, they had decided to fly to New York instead. Leaving Newfoundland that evening, the aviators were in wireless communication with Cape Race and their conversation was overheard by the operators of R.34. Just after eight o'clock came the news, intercepted by the airship and passed eagerly to the crew, that Jack Dempsey had defeated Jess Willard in the third round of their fight for the world heavyweight boxing championship. No one had expected a different result and the stowaway, Ballantyne, himself a keen bantam-weight boxer, had been unable to find a single taker when he had offered an even £5 on the challenger. Unhappily, the Handley-Page biplane fared no better than Willard, for later that night its signals ceased abruptly and were not resumed. Saturday morning, R.34's fourth day in the air, dawned with concern for the Handley-Page adding to her crew's increased worry about their own chances. Long before dawn, strong adverse winds were beating against the ship and holding her back as she thrust slowly southward. To the west, across a narrow strip of Nova Scotia, was the long inlet of the Bay of Fundy and towards this Major Scott now steered, seeking to save his ship from the constant buffeting. Five hundred gallons of fuel were left now and the ship was flying very light. To escape the gales, she flew only 800 ft above the never-ending forests, forced down by her elevators and inclined so steeply forward that she bore all the signs of heading for an imminent crash. More than three hours were spent travelling in this fashion through a warm, fragrant morning during which the all-pervading scent of pine rose to the thirty-one men passing closely over the treetops. Once an eagle was seen, and on another occasion the airship was flying so low that the sharp barking of a lonely dog could be heard distinctly above the dull roaring of the engines. The cat, Wopsie, undoubtedly heard it too, for the crew members off watch were amused to see her arch her back and bristle at the sound.

With R.34's load now reduced considerably by the consumption of fuel, the ship possessed an excessive and unwanted buoyancy. To remove this, she was taken up above pressure height for a short while, in order that hydrogen might be blown off equally from all the gasbags. After reaching the Bay of Fundy at midday, two of the engines were kept constantly out of use, for maximum economy. Such a restriction was only a palliative and Major Scott had now to face the distinct possibility of having to stop short of even his revised objective. There remained the various alternatives of landing at Boston, anchoring with the sea-drogue or being taken in tow by a warship. The first two courses would be only intervals for refuelling, but the third meant the galling prospect of R.34 being towed ignominiously into New York harbour, there to be released to complete only the last few yards under her own power. Major Scott had no intention of employing any of these measures, except in the last extremity, but the likelihood had to be admitted and he contacted both Boston and New York to request that a destroyer should stand by as a precautionary measure. The message was relayed through the station at Bar Harbor, where an operator carelessly prefixed it with 'Rush', the American sign for urgency, so misleading

53

Looking aft from the port window of the forward gondola. (Fleet Air Arm Museum)

everyone into thinking that matters were really desperate. Anticipating the worst, the U.S. Navy responded by sending the two warships *Bancroft* and *Stevens* to cruise off Cape Cod, while Major Fuller drove to Boston in case R.34 should be obliged to land there. Back in England, the message was seized upon by the newspapers, who gave it considerable publicity and caused needless anxiety to the relatives of the airmen.

In the meantime, the airship carried on down the Bay of Fundy, the crew cheered by better news of the Handley-Page biplane, which had landed safely in the streets of the little seaport town of Parrsborough, after engine failure. At first the weather was much calmer and R.34 made progress enough to raise the hopes of all on board — hopes that began to fall when a thunderstorm, clearly visible in the north-west, came rolling down the bay after them. The ship was at once swung to port under full power and at first it seemed that the worst violence of the wind had been evaded. Then the helmsman, Leading Aircraftman John Forteath, pointed to the compass card, which was spinning madly as the electrical disturbance of the storm came nearer. Lieutenant Luck scrambled up the ladder into the keel to fetch Major Scott, who was enjoying a brief sleep. The captain hurried back to take charge as the ship was caught on the eastern fringes of the squall and shaken mercilessly in its grip. Frightening moments followed; moments when the airship fell several hundred feet in one sickening drop or pitched steeply to almost incredible angles at which the engines could not function properly. Cutting out momentarily, they burst back immediately into life with an explosion of flame from the exhaust-pipes which could be seen clearly even by the men inside the keel. In the forward car, the medical stores, including a bottle of brandy, were scattered all over the floor, and throughout the ship any loose objects were sent sliding

54

into corners. Everyone clung on grimly and no one was hurt. Only Lieutenant Shotter was caught unprepared; he happened to be taking a rare rest period at this crucial instant, lying down dangerously near to the open drogue hatch in the bows. As the airship tilted forward, he slipped headlong and saved himself only by hooking his foot round a providential girder.

Soon the airship resumed her correct course and the storm rumbled away into the south-east, to be succeeded by a period of calm which lasted throughout the afternoon and into the evening. While the dusk closed gently in, the smooth sea reflected the sombre tints of fading daylight and the keening of the wind in the rigging wires sounded quiet and low-pitched. Suddenly and inexplicably came more violent bumps and some of the fiercest buffeting of the whole voyage. At times, R.34 started to rear upright before falling sharply forward into a steep, nose-down position. Sometimes she surged abruptly upwards, hovered momentarily, and then dropped back again with jolting suddenness. For a short while the airship was like a playful whale disporting itself. The illusion was increased when looking back from the control-cabin, for it was even possible to see her tail flex under the strain of her antics.

The powerful winds which had caused these extraordinary contortions had come suddenly and swiftly out of cloudless skies and were the more terrifying in that no warning of their approach had been discerned, except an abrupt and startling rise in the air temperature, followed by an equally sudden fall. Overhead, the moon shone brightly and steadily, while far below, the surface of the sea remained glassy and untroubled. Even Lieutenant Harris could only guess the cause of these new disturbances and he provisionally attributed them to errant currents from the Gulf Stream intermingling with much colder

R.34 in flight. (Imperial War Museum)

waters coming down from the north. This explanation did nothing to mitigate the effects and the crew of R.34 could only hang on as the recurrent onslaughts slowly diminished in violence and eventually died away altogether. Between these angry squalls and continuing after they ceased, came a slight but favourable wind which sped the airship on her journey southwards. By midnight it began to seem that Long Island was attainable without an intermediate stop, after all, even although much invaluable fuel had been consumed in coping with the gales.

In the small hours of Sunday morning there was an exchange of messages with the U.S. Navy at their Washington headquarters, during which Major Scott reluctantly confirmed that he would stop at Montauk for refuelling and asked for a landing-party to be sent there. At least there was now no chance of an even more premature finish to the voyage, for overnight the following wind had increased in strength and the ship made good speed over a calm sea. Massachusetts was passed serenely by and just before breakfast, Long Island loomed on the clear horizon. Major Scott held a hurried conference with Lieutenant Shotter, who shook his head doubtfully when he heard what was required. Nevertheless, he quickly assembled a search party and equipped them with all the spare jars, containers and cooking-pots he could lay hold of. Then he took them round the ship's fuel tanks, more than eighty in all, examining, draining and pumping each one to salvage the last available drops of petrol. There seemed to be just enough and after hearing the Engineer Officer's report, Major Scott made his decision: R.34 would try to go straight through to Hazelhurst Field, Mineola, their original destination.

It was twenty minutes to eight, local time, when Montauk Naval Air Station was passed. There could be no going back now and Major Scott doubtless held his favourite gold charm tightly and hoped fervently that no more emergencies would arise. Petrol was not the only commodity in short supply; all the drinking water and most of the food had gone, and the lightened airship was held aloft by a much reduced volume of gas. During the long four-and-a-half days' travel, much of the hydrogen had imperceptibly disappeared, by expansion, natural leakage and deliberate valving. Tightly embracing the keel-corridor at the commencement of the flight, the gasbags had slowly loosened their grip, and the crew looked out from the keel at a concavity of girders, hung with the slack drapes of cotton fabric.

Throughout the ship during the last hour, men struggled to make themselves and their clothes presentable for the landing. By nine o'clock, Mineola came into view, with crowds of people waiting to welcome the airship, and thousands more still streaming out from New York to the airfield. Enormous car-parks were already nearly full and a military band played in front of a specially erected grandstand. As the crew, their personal preparations completed or cut short, went to their landing stations, there came a last message from the ground. Major Fuller, who was to have organized the landing-party, had not yet returned from Boston and the servicemen were commanded by Captain Samuel Moore of the U.S. Army and Lieutenant Hoyt of the U.S. Navy. Apart from the eight English airmen, their men were all American soldiers or sailors, who were totally unaccustomed to handling large rigid airships. Many, indeed, had been hastily assembled only a short while earlier, in place of those mistakenly sent to Montauk and not yet returned. All in all, there was considerable confusion on the ground as R.34 circled overhead. Major Scott was unwilling to trust his precious craft to such inexperienced hands, so it was clear that someone must parachute down and take charge of the landing and mooring arrangements. General Maitland would have been delighted to do this, but for the senior officer to descend in such a manner might have appeared ostentatious, and ruefully he allowed Major Pritchard to volunteer. Understandably, as he was about to become the first man to reach America by air, Major Pritchard was anxious to present a smart appearance. Like everyone else, he was badly in need of a shave, and so some hot water was quickly obtained for him from one of the engine radiators. With his shave hastily completed, he was helped through the window of the forward car by two of his fellow officers and descended safely to the ground — the only foreigner ever to arrive in the United States by parachute.

After one more circuit of the airfield, R.34 came slowly and gently down to earth. It was 9.54 a.m. local time and 1.54 p.m. Greenwich Mean Time. The outward journey had taken 108 hours, 12 minutes, which was a world endurance record, breaking that set by NS.11 a few months earlier. There were only about 140 gallons of petrol left on board, sufficient for about two hours' flying on reduced power.

R.34 at Mineola. (Author's collection)

CHAPTER 8

New York

The United States had long been preparing for the arrival of R.34. The original hope had been that she would arrive on the Fourth of July: a fitting spectacle for Independence Day to be set alongside the Dempsey-Willard title fight. Although the unexpectedly protracted flight had prevented this exciting juxtaposition, the airship's approach was the signal for many demonstrations of welcome and regard, both organised and spontaneous. Nothing like R.34 had ever been seen over the American continent before. She was far bigger than the small blimps which comprised the United States airship fleet and the sight of her vast, streamlined hull floating majestically over Long Island brought thousands out to Mineola by car, tram or cycle, to see her close at hand on that fine summer morning. The U.S. Navy had prepared for the arrival of the British airship with a lavish disregard for expense, and more than a thousand men from the Air Service were on hand to provide a handling-party. While many of them were experienced with airships, few, if any, had moored or handled large rigids and it was intended that one of the British officers, preferably Major Fuller, should take command on the arrival of R.34. Many cylinders of gas and several thousand gallons of petrol were stored in readiness, special grandstands were erected and viewing areas for the public roped off. The U.S. Army were also involved and five hundred military policemen stood by to control the crowds and to supervise the large car-parks which had been marked out near the airfield. So far did the Americans' caution extend that all aeroplanes were forbidden to come within five miles of Hazelhurst Field or of the airship as she approached.

One of the few Americans among the landing-party with any personal knowledge of British airships was Frank Peckham, who had served as a volunteer with the Royal Navy. When word was received that R.34 was to stop at Montauk, Peckham was ordered to take a party and go to meet her there. Several hundred men, together with supplies of hydrogen and petrol, were rushed out to the eastern tip of Long Island, where they reached the field just in time to see the airship pass straight over their heads on her way to Mineola. Peckham immediately turned his lorries and chased the airship all the way back. He arrived barely in time to see a parachute descending from the still circling R.34.

Major Pritchard came down safely, if rather heavily, at some distance from the marked landing-place. He rose to his feet to confront several reporters who had dashed across with pencils, notebooks and questions at the ready. On being asked what were his first impressions of America, he dealt with the fatuous query by pointing to the ground and replying laconically, 'Hard!', then he climbed on to the pillion of a motorcycle which had driven up to fetch him over to the landing-party. The Major's answer was insufficiently dramatic for the Americans and it subsequently appeared in newspapers as 'Dry!': an alleged allusion to Prohibition.

U.S. soldiers watch as R.34 descends steeply to earth at Mineola. (Royal Aeronautical Society)

While Major Pritchard was introducing himself to Lieutenant Hoyt and explaining what was required, R.34 completed another circuit over Hazelhurst Field and then Major Scott manoeuvred her carefully into position for a slow descent. Gas was valved, water ballast was released from the tail, and the long trail rope snaked from the bows. The airship, all forward movement at an end, nosed gradually down to earth and into the hands of the landing party, with her engines still and her propellers safely in the horizontal position.

Then the band struck up 'God save the King' and the forward gondola bumped lightly on to the turf. As soon as the ship was made fast, the crew stepped out to all the uninhibited exuberance of an American public occasion: cheers, music, speeches and loud congratulations. Many naval and military officers were waiting to greet them, including Lieutenant Little of the U.S. Navy Air Service, who had been one of the two men who had jumped for safety when the C.5 blimp blew away into the Atlantic a few months earlier. Along with several others present, he had flown on convoy and patrol duties in British waters during the war and was known personally to many of the Englishmen. For the benefit of the newspapermen present, Vice-Admiral Gleaves of the U.S. Navy made a formal speech of welcome, to which General Maitland replied, and then the crew faced up to the inevitable battery of photographers and newsreel men. This first reception was kept brief and soon the crew were making use of the hot baths and showers which, like so many other facilities, had been supplied especially for their benefit. R.34 was handed over to the

The two stowaways of R.34, A.C.2 William Ballantyne and Wopsie, meet the American Press. (Press Association)

U.S. Navy and the crew were taken away in a procession of cars to the Garden City Hotel, where a splendid luncheon had been laid on, also by the hospitable sailors. Here they were joined by Major Fuller, returned from Boston, Commander Read of the NC-4 flying boat and many other senior or well-known British and United States servicemen. While the citizens of New York continued to throng Hazelhurst Field for a sight of the moored airship, the airmen themselves relaxed in comfort. Speeches were made, wine drunk, a marvellous variety of foods eaten and a seal set on the celebrations by the arrival of a congratulatory telegram from King George V. Afterwards, everyone went outside for an informal press conference where the neatness of the Englishmen's appearance was much admired, as well as their determinedly British under-statements. Major Pritchard particularly endeared himself to the reporters and his bland, 'I can't see what all the howl is about!' was widely quoted in the local newspapers.

After this, the officers left for the Ritz-Carlton Hotel, where rooms had been provided for them by the American Aero Club, and the lower ranks were driven off by U.S. petty-officers to humbler quarters. Even at the Ritz-Carlton the officers were unable to escape the attention of reporters and photographers, who followed them right into their bedrooms on one of the highest floors. Lieutenant Shotter, for one, was more than tired; he was exhausted. Having slept only in brief snatches since leaving Scotland, he had kept awake through the last crucial hours by the dubious means of dosing himself with Lieutenant Luck's aspirins. Walking across to open a window, he staggered with fatigue and so gave a splendid headline to one of the newspapers: 'Gallant Englishman flies the Atlantic and faints at sight of height.' His friends did not allow him to forget this indignity for a long time.

During the next few days all the crew were treated to constant and lavish generosity, when most of the men were given leave to enjoy the New Yorkers' hospitality to the full. Everywhere they were wined, dined and bombarded with invitations to formal functions and private parties. Cars and drivers were found to carry them around, presents were pressed upon them and when they entered public rooms, everybody stood up. It was a heady experience and everyone enjoyed himself to the full in the brief time available. The pleasures of fame were not without their accompanying dangers, as one of R.34's officers found to his cost. Strolling into the street one morning for some fresh air, he was mobbed by eager admirers, who made off with his white hat-cover and three of his tunic buttons. Further embarrassment was prevented only by the arrival of the police, who delivered a polite reprimand on the hazards of walking unescorted. William Ballantyne's exploit appealed especially to the Americans and he was interviewed by journalists anxious for his story. Photographs of him holding the cat — both stowaways — featured in many newspapers and Wopsie (called Jazz by the Americans) even received the honour of a poem in the *New York Herald*. Worthy of McGonagall himself, it included the verse:

> *I have gone where no other cat has gone,*
> *(I lick my paws and I rub my ears),*
> *Who have roamed the sky before the dawn,*
> *As I've longed to do for the years and the years.*

Adulation could go no further.

General Maitland found time to remedy the toothache which had been troubling him since leaving England and it was typical of the treatment accorded to all the airmen that the dentist he consulted asked only for the Englishman's autograph: a form of currency that paid for almost anything. Not everyone was able to give himself up to the pleasures of the moment and for some of the crew the interval before the return flight was a hectic period of checking, greasing and overhauling. Lieutenant Shotter and his men turned again to their engines, cleaning carburettors and magnetos as well as replacing half of the one hundred and twenty spark plugs. Fortunately, no real repairs were necessary and, with the oil supply replenished, they were soon finished. The propellers had accumulated a thick coating of engine oil, but this was removed free of charge by a local firm, who also repaired the canvas covering which had been torn over the Atlantic.

R.34 herself was in good shape. At night she was moored by the 'three wire' system, which involved leading three cables from widely separated anchorages to a point beneath the bows of the airship, whose lift then kept the pyramid taut. During the day she was pulled down and held by the united efforts of the American handling-party, but even for these hefty sailors it was an arduous task and one which had to be undertaken in relays. In the absence of a suitably sized hangar, there was no alternative, of course, as the essential maintenance and servicing had to be carried out on the ground.

On Sunday, the water-ballast was renewed to compensate for the increased lift produced by the midday sun, only to be hurriedly released again when a storm blew up. There had not yet been time to replenish the gas and in the heavy rain the ship could not be raised safely off the ground in time. Before the gale blew itself out, the handling rail on the after car was knocked completely off against the ground. After this, the gassing was finished as quickly as possible and at ten o'clock the airship at last flew clear and the weary handling-party could be sent away. The bright sunshine of the next morning again caused gas expansion and by eight o'clock the airship was tugging strongly at her moorings in a stiff breeze. When the handling-party tried to haul her down for the maintenance work to commence, they found the job almost beyond them. Men were lifted bodily into the air and dropped heavily back again as the ship rocked violently from side to side. More men were sent for, to add their weight to the taut ropes, and together they managed to keep her from breaking away. Nevertheless, the strain on the ship's structure was considerable and in the end it was the casting holding the main mooring point at the bows which gave way. The airship's nose jerked upwards and for one frantic moment it seemed that she might tear herself loose and float away. Then the casting slid backwards and jammed itself firmly and fortunately in the shackle, where it stuck fast. Although the actual damage was not great, news of the mishap brought Major Scott back from his hotel in a state of considerable anxiety. There was a large gash in the outer cover under the nose, about three yards long, but no vital girders or framework were affected. Major Scott fully realised what might have happened, however, and he hurried along the preparations for departure. Once the ship was down it was possible to make temporary repairs without too much trouble and in the evening, with the trim correctly adjusted, she was again allowed to ride freely at her moorings, bathed silver by the surrounding search-lights. As always, the night air chilled the gas and the airship began to wallow heavily. Only about thirty men were on watch, a completely insufficient number to handle R.34 normally, but they managed to pull the tail down far enough for a man to climb into the after car and thence into the keel. Twice he did this to release ballast and the ship rode out the night without further incident.

On the Tuesday she was again pulled down for the final maintenance work to be carried out and it was even possible to allow a few privileged visitors on board. For the remainder of the numerous spectators there was only the chance to stare and the opportunity of studying R.34's statistical data in a small handbook, price one dollar, hastily produced for the occasion by the enterprising Bracegirdle Chowder Society. Many of those who came to look at the airship were surprised to see no British uniforms among the men crowded round her. Such an impression of idleness was misleading and a result of the Britons' restricted supply of clothing. Many of them had been loaned uniforms by the U.S. Army and so were now indistinguishable from the American servicemen among whom they were now working. That night was the airship's last at Mineola and, as always when correctly moored and trimmed, she behaved with lady-like docility and dignity.

Except for the final gassing and last-minute servicing, R.34 was now ready and prepared. Before the ship left, however, other requirements had to be met and other arrangements made, apart from the merely technical considerations. Many special letters were collected for distribution in England, mostly in reply to those which had been brought over in the airship. Lieutenant-Colonel Lucas had also rather rashly offered to obtain rum for the return journey, evidently misled by the way the onset of Prohibition was so blatantly ignored by almost everyone. National Prohibition was not actually set to begin until the following January, when the sale of liquor would become illegal, but only a week before R.34's arrival, in preparation, the manufacture of all alcoholic drinks had officially ceased. There had been consequent stockpiling by many people over the last few days and although wine, brandy or beer could be purchased with only slight difficulty, rum was another matter altogether and Lieutenant-Colonel Lucas was eventually obliged to admit defeat.

Major Scott had to consider how his crew would be reorganized in the light of the experiences of the outward journey. In view of the unexpectedly severe strain imposed on his engineers, he decided to increase their number by two and Lieutenant Shotter chose Flight-Sergeants Turner and Angus from the party sent ahead under Lieutenant-Colonel Lucas and Major Fuller. In their place, Major Scott left behind a W.T. operator, Aircraftman Edwards, and also one rigger, the stowaway, Aircraftman Ballantyne, who would return by sea with the ground-crew. Lieutenant-Commander Lansdowne also was to make only the one crossing; for the eastward voyage he was succeeded by Lieutenant-Colonel Hensley, who represented the U.S. Army as his predecessor had the U.S. Navy.

The cat, Wopsie, was again included in the ranks, after being in some danger of becoming permanently American. It is reliably reported that L. A. C. Graham was offered a thousand dollars for her by a wealthy actress, but refused indignantly. This means that he turned down far more than a year's pay for his now famous pet: an almost incredible sacrifice which the lady mitigated somewhat by the present of a gold-plated collar.

One other former member of the crew was sadly lacking from the voyage home. Someone, unversed in the ways of such creatures, had released the two carrier pigeons for some much-needed exercise. Although one was now safely back in its cage, the other had somehow escaped and had been last seen heading determinedly away from the airship. Many presents which were received could not be taken on board for the weight, and had to be sent home by sea. One, however, was allowed by general consent: a new gramophone and a fresh supply of records. The old one was carelessly flung out and was immediately dismembered by avid souvenir hunters who had already helped themselves to insecure parts of the after engine-car and anything else left unguarded.

On Wednesday afternoon, the petrol, oil, food and other provisions were loaded, with the intention of starting for home at dawn the next morning. Round about nine o'clock, however, with Major Scott and General Maitland at yet another dinner in Garden City, a message came from Washington warning of approaching high winds, probably amounting to gale force. Lieutenant Harris fully realised the dangers of further delay and he telephoned the captain at once. The crew were hurriedly assembled and by the time Scott and Maitland returned, the final task of gassing the ship had begun. Held down by long lines of servicemen leaning backwards over the mooring-ropes, like tug-of-war contestants, the airship rolled heavily but safely. There were four hundred men, weighing perhaps thirty tons altogether, to hold her fast so that, providing the ropes themselves did not break free, she was secure. Other members of the handling-party struggled to keep the forward car from dashing itself against the ground as the overshadowing hull swayed ominously in the gusts of freshening wind. Standing in front of the ship, where he commanded a view of these activities, was the American officer in charge. Holding a megaphone to his lips, he exercised some degree of control — shouting instructions to each line of sweating men as they relaxed or strained overmuch. A thick, white pipe carried hydrogen into the gasbags with a loud hissing noise that rendered inaudible the comments of the engineers leaning out of the gondola windows. By eleven o'clock, the whole busy scene had calmed somewhat. Not so the weather, and the wind whistled more loudly and insistently through the wires and rigging. Major Scott had watched his men climb into their places, and now he also ascended the rope ladder to the control-cabin. The sight of his stocky figure at the forward window showed that all was now ready for departure. Only General Maitland was still missing and he soon clambered up to take his position by the side of the captain.

While the last few cubic feet of hydrogen were distending the gasbags, the crew experienced their last and unofficial act of American generosity. A man pushed his way through the jostling crowds with a wooden box on his shoulder. Allowed by the military police to approach the airship, he dashed forward to hand up his burden into the forward gondola. It was the much coveted and hitherto unobtainable case of rum!

A few moments later the hissing of gas ceased and the pipe was hauled clear. Through the megaphone boomed the command, 'Spectators keep silent!' The shouting, cheering and farewells sank obediently into quiet, disturbed only by the whining of wind, the creak of rigging and the low murmuring of many voices. Major Scott put his hand to the telegraph, which rang faintly in the ears of those watching. One by one the engines started into life, purring smoothly in the cool air. Pausing a little while for them to warm up, he raised his megaphone in one hand, waved goodbye with the other, and then shouted a firm, 'Let go all!' Four hundred servicemen released the mooring ropes as one man and R.34 rose sharply, cleanly and majestically into the night sky. The time was exactly six minutes to midnight local time, or 3.54 a.m. G.M.T.

The gasbags are replenished at Mineola. (Press Association)

CHAPTER 9

Eastward

A heartening repeat of past experience followed R.34 into the air: a great burst of cheering from thousands of spectators, ground-crew and officials which could be clearly heard by the British airmen. The wind was now gusting at nearly 30 m.p.h. and there had been no opportunity to correct the trim before leaving, so the efficient take-off was all the more creditable. The ship flew almost level, only slightly down by the stern at first, and although rather less petrol was being carried this time, the prospect of strong prevailing winds in her favour made the outlook for R.34's return journey very encouraging.

As a gesture of gratitude for the almost overwhelming hospitality they had all received, Major Scott had agreed to fly low over New York, that the ship might be picked out by searchlights and seen by as many people as possible. Crossing from Long Island at about 1,000 ft above sea level, she gingerly approached the Manhattan skyline, lit up by innumerable signs, advertisements and street lights. Nobody in R.34's control-cabin was very sure what was the exact height of the skyscrapers and so the ship was prudently taken up another 500 ft to be on the safe side. In fact, at the former altitude she would have been low enough to be in some danger among the uncertain air-currents above the city. At that time, the tallest skyscraper was the six-year-old Woolworth Building, 790 ft high, and there were others not much lower. When R.34 drew closer to the centre of the metropolis, she was driven up yet higher to a secure 2,000 ft where, floating only three times her own length above the streets, she was fully comparable in size to the vertical monsters that rose up beneath her keel.

From all around, the probing white fingers of the searchlights crept through the darkness, crossing and recrossing to seek her out. Suddenly, somewhere above Fifth Avenue, a brilliant glare shone through the windows of the gondola and others soon followed the lead of the first, to attach themselves to the vast silver expanse of the hull. Despite the time — approaching one o'clock in the morning — there were many thousands of sightseers still in the street to cheer the airship on her way. The crew looked down at their upturned faces, garishly illuminated in the multicoloured lights as they waved wildly and mouthed unheard farewells. In spite of the bumpy air-currents over the city, the ship kept remarkably steady and after ten minutes of floodlit progress she slipped from the searchlights' hold and turned eastward again towards the open sea.

The wind at her tail was strong and constant, and she headed out over the Atlantic at a surface speed of nearly 80 m.p.h. Two large depressions had been reported, centred near Newfoundland and Iceland. By skirting the southern fringes, Major Scott hoped to repeat his manoeuvre of the week before, but this time to greater effect, and to use the westerly airflow to speed R.34 on her voyage home.

Good progress was made throughout the night, which continued dark and windy. In the

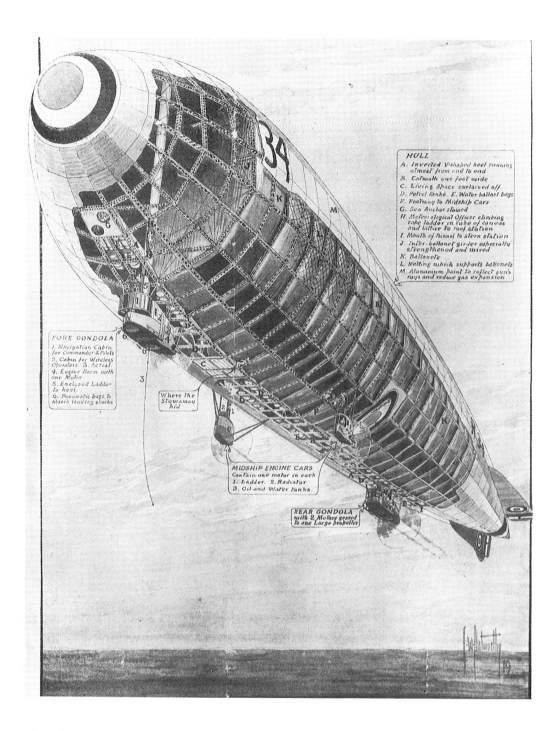

An artist's impression of R.34 which appeared in the Graphic on 12 July 1919, while the airship was still on her homeward journey. (Royal Aeronautical Society)

blackness of the small hours the Nantucket lightship signalled the last contact with the American continent and by breakfast the ship was more than four hundred miles out from New York. Attaining a speed of nearly 90 m.p.h. with the forward engine rested, R.34 was being swept along at an exhilarating rate by the prevailing winds, just as Alcock and Brown had been pushed to success earlier in the year. So well, in fact, did their present swiftness compare with the hard slog of the westward flight, that General Maitland and Major Scott discussed together the possibility of varying the pre-arranged schedule and flying first over London before returning to East Fortune. In the circumstances they had no difficulty in deciding upon this more exciting arrangement, travelling 'from the capital of one country to the capital of the other' as General Maitland, enthusiastically but inaccurately, recorded it in his log. Below the ship, rough seas with steep waves and deep troughs could be seen, but the upper air-currents flowed with calm smoothness, bearing the dirigible along with neither pitching nor rolling to upset her dignified stability. Visibility was also very good and Major Cooke was able to take accurate observations of the sun's angle to the sea horizon and so fix their position with easy accuracy. During the whole of the outward voyage he had found only three occasions when this had been possible.

Towards the end of the afternoon, the wind eased considerably as the airship began to move away from the first depression. While still hoping to obtain help from the second, more northerly one, Lieutenant Harris was able to assure everyone that if the wind returned in force, it could be blowing only in the desired direction. With the prevailing weather conditions, a headwind was impossible.

At a quarter past six on that same evening occurred an event unique in the entire voyage. Save for coastal shipping, no vessels had been seen in the open sea, although wireless messages had frequently proved them to be in the airship's vicinity. Now happened the only such sighting, a few miles away on the starboard beam: a five-masted schooner dipping slowly through the waves. For minutes only, the ships that passed in the night kept anachronistic company. Then R.34 drew swiftly ahead and the schooner became lost in the desolation of the sea: the last as well as the first ocean-going vessel to be thus spotted by the airmen. Not for the only time they remembered and marvelled at the luck of Mackenzie-Grieve and Hawker, that they had found someone to save them in the midst of this watery wilderness.

The second night passed as an uneventful repetition of the first, until early on Friday morning one of the engines failed completely. It was the starboard of the two in the after car and the damage was caused when one of the engineers slipped and fell against the clutch lever, so freeing the engine. Under load at the time and with the governor gear disconnected, it raced to destruction as connecting-rods fractured under the suddenly increased stress. No repair would be possible until the ship docked and although she could continue safely on the remaining four engines, there would be more strain on these and no reserve of power for emergencies. In the different conditions posed by this handicap, the idea of flying directly to London had to be abandoned reluctantly and the necessary alterations to the ship's course were made at once.

By now the eternal cloudscapes of the North Atlantic had come rolling back to cover the sea: not the level carpet of the westward voyage but a mass of ever-changing hummocks, cliffs and cottonwool valleys. Bringing the ship down to 600 ft to get back into clear air, Major Scott discovered that there was a strong contrary wind at that low height. The ship's course lay over the warm Gulf Stream and the proximity of colder waters to the north apparently caused this local variation to the prevailing westerly airstream. Ascending again above cloud-level to 3,000 ft, R.34 regained the favourable wind corridor and continued on her way. Even stronger winds probably blew at higher altitudes, but with the need to conserve buoyancy, Major Scott preferred not to lose gas through expansion until the weight of petrol had been further reduced. The long afternoon passed away without sight of the sea, lost somewhere beneath the obscuring clouds, and Major Cooke was once more obliged to climb the 80 ft ladder to the machine-gun platform to fix the ship's position from the unreliable cloud horizon. Without sight of the sea it was also difficult to estimate speed or wind-direction, and again Major Scott drove R.34 plunging down through the mist. From nearly 4,000 ft she dropped slowly through five separate layers of cloud, each of which formed the floor and the roof to a shallow world of windswept emptiness. Even at the lowest level of about 900 ft, the ocean was still invisible and Major Scott dared not risk descending further. Instead, he brought the ship back to her former height, where for some minutes she sailed through a mountainous landscape of dazzling white hills silhouetted against the blue sky. The reflected glare of the sun shone into eyes grown accustomed to gloom and the men in the control-cabin shaded their brows against the dazzle. Such pleasant conditions could not last, however, and before long the ship re-entered the grey mist, where rain, cold and damp soon added to the general dark unpleasantness. Another increase in altitude failed to bring the ship into better weather and she returned to the 3,000 ft level to continue her course by dead reckoning. All windows were shut and the crew huddled into hammocks or flying-suits to keep warm.

To increase the captain's anxiety came bad news from Lieutenant Shotter. The forward engine was performing erratically and had to be stopped for attention while the ship thrust forward on barely half her total horsepower. The trouble, however, proved to be only several broken valve springs, and within two hours the engine was running normally again. While the engineers evidently had much to contend with, their lot was at least better than on the outward flight. Not only were there two more men to share the work, but the problem of sleeplessness was no longer so acute. Each man going off watch was issued with a tot of rum and so slept off the effect of continuous engine roar. Away from the engine-cars the noise was far less obtrusive and on that Friday evening, with rain howling mournfully in the rigging, it was difficult for those not directly concerned to hear the engines at all.

Major Cooke had become increasingly anxious to know how far the airship was keeping to her correct course and in an attempt to obtain a rough estimate of speed and drift he dropped overboard a calcium flare. He watched it fall away behind the airship and ignite as it struck the water: a pinpoint of light dwindling quickly to extinction dead astern and providing some indication of high speed and little drift. At least R.34 was drawing nearer home all the while, for messages from Clifden Wireless Station on the Irish west coast were now picked up without difficulty, and later that night, East Fortune could again be heard, albeit very faintly. Two more flares, three hours later, revealed a slight drift to the south and enabled a corrected course to be steered. At around midnight, a message was received from the Air Ministry, relayed by Clifden. To everyone's surprise, R.34 was instructed to proceed to Pulham in Norfolk, ostensibly because of bad weather at East Fortune. This was a considerable disappointment to the lower ranks in particular, as it postponed their homecoming to the families who awaited them in Scotland, and when a favourable weather report was obtained directly from East Fortune a few hours later, Major Scott asked the Air Ministry for permission to revert to the original destination. Despite the fact that this would have saved the handicapped airship some four hours of flying time, his request was turned down flatly and it was towards Norfolk that R.34 eventually headed.

No reason was ever given for the abrupt change of mind by the Air Ministry and no obvious explanation can be advanced. However, the restricted funds of a peacetime defence budget had already provoked opposition to the spending of large sums on expensive dirigibles. It has been conjectured that those who supported only an aeroplane programme may have contrived the altered destination in order to avoid the publicity of the great welcome that was being planned at East Fortune. Pulham, by contrast, was comparatively isolated and probably only Royal Air Force personnel would be present, so ensuring the minimum fuss and excitement. If this theory is true — and it accords with later policy developments and the shabby treatment soon meted out to everyone on board — then the manoeuvre was an unworthy affront to servicemen who could neither disobey nor complain.

With sunrise there soon came clearer weather and the opportunity once more to check the ship's position by sextant; she was less than a thousand miles from home and on a true course. A gradual slackening of the westerly wind had occurred since the previous evening and now the estimated surface-speed was reduced to around 40 m.p.h., the normal still-air cruising speed. Plenty of petrol remained in the tanks and even without full engine-power the homeward voyage was proving to be much easier than the outward, as had been anticipated. Although cold, Saturday's weather was generally clear, but a wind soon sprang up from the north-east, hindering progress and bringing the inevitable mist clouds in its train.

Around midday, one clear patch extended to the horizon in all directions and from 5,000 ft up the observers in the airship could look down on an estimated 20,000 square miles of salt water — each one without rock, ship or sign of life. No more convincing proof of the awful emptiness of the Atlantic could have been proffered. Five hours later, two trawlers were spotted eight miles or so away to the south: a sight to cause excitement not for its intrinsic interest, but because the presence of such coastal vessels confirmed the navigator's calculation that land was close. Another two hours were to pass, however, before the only American on board, Lieutenant-Colonel Hensley, finally caught the first glimpse of Europe. Altering course to make landfall, R.34 flew over the Irish coast near the same small islands which had been seen first by Alcock and Brown when they emerged at length out of the Atlantic fogs.

At eight o'clock in the evening, the airship climbed to cross the Irish mountains. Between tawny peaks the setting sun shone across a green land of woods, valleys and fields whose fresh variety was a relief to the eyes after the dull tints of sea, sky and cloud. Flying to meet the airship from Castlebar came a small biplane, which circled excitedly around like a very small dog worrying a large and placid cow. Then the pilot and passenger waved a welcome before leaving the dirigible to make her way over flat country towards Belfast and the Irish Sea. Uneventfully, R.34 moved steadily eastward during the night, to cross the English coast near Liverpool, where long lines of lights glittered in the murky waters of the Mersey. Then she made her way past Nottingham and Derby towards Norfolk and Pulham. Once again the W.T. operators were kept busy transcribing messages of congratulation as the ship neared the end of her voyage. The Prime Minister, Lloyd George, and the Secretary of State for War and Air, Winston Churchill, were only two of many who hastened to join in the chorus of praise.

To the very end of the flight, the engines continued to give trouble and Pulham was reached with only two still running. In the other cars the propellers were released to rotate in the airstream so that the airship might make a more impressive spectacle as she

R.34 arrives over the airfield at Pulham. The tank was used as a tractor to pull open the hangar doors.
(Press Association)

R.34 comes into land at Pulham. (Central Press)

approached the airfield. Then she circled the field twice while Major Scott signalled to the landing-party by Aldis lamp. There were four hundred men in all, under the command of Captain Cochrane, and they had made their preparations over an hour before R.34 came in sight. Also in attendance was a rather small R.A.F. band, hastily assembled from those musicians who were not on weekend leave. Except for some reporters and officials, there were not many other spectators to welcome the airmen in such a remote corner at such an early hour. The contrast between their triumphal arrival in the United States and their present rather tepid reception was already obvious, even from the air.

Dipping her bows gently, R.34 dived into the slight wind. Then her engines cut out as the trail rope whistled down into the hands of the landing-party, who tugged the airship enthusiastically towards the ground. She was coming in rather nose-heavy and to adjust the trim Major Scott emptied a bag of forward water-ballast. According to one account, he chose an unfortunate moment and the band, standing directly underneath the bows and just striking up 'See The Conquering Hero Comes', were doused in the unexpected downpour. With truly British phlegm, they continued playing while the airship completed her descent.

It was 6.57 a.m. G.M.T. (7.57 British Summer Time) and the return journey had been completed in three days, three hours and three minutes. Since leaving East Fortune, R.34 had covered 7,420 miles (6,444 nautical miles) at an average airspeed of about 43 m.p.h. (37.1 knots). The surface speeds of the outward and homeward flights were 28.9 knots and 44.2 knots respectively: a difference caused by the strong winds of the North Atlantic.

R.34 in the hangar at Pulham. Major Scott reads the telegram from King George V. (Press Association)

CHAPTER 10

Anti-climax

Captain Cochrane bellowed instructions through his megaphone and within moments R.34 was firmly in the grip of the handlers and being led with disciplined care towards the hangar. Away to one side of the airfield was a high, steel mooring-post to which was tethered one of the old rigid airships, No.24. But no one paid any attention to this obsolete craft as slowly, stern first, R.34 was brought into the hangar alongside her sister-ship, R.33. Only then, protected from the gales and fastened securely down, could her voyage be said to have ended safely. As Major Scott stepped out of the control-cabin, he was handed a telegram from the King, which said:

I heartily congratulate you all on your safe return home after the completion of your memorable and, indeed, unique transatlantic air voyage. — George R & I.

There was still much to be done and the excitement of adventure gave way to the prosaic duties of administration; for reports had to be written, inspections made and a multiplicity of details attended to. On the outward journey, R.34 had taken a letter from the editor of *The Times* to his counterpart of the Philadelphia *Public Ledger*. On her return home, she brought an answer and also several copies of the American newspaper. The reply was handed in to *The Times* special correspondent from the airship gondola, even before the docking was finished, and the newspapers were delivered without delay. One was addressed to the King at Buckingham Palace and he received it at half-past two that afternoon. Some other copies were put on sale in London and sold briskly to souvenir hunters. The other matters were less urgent and for most members of the airship crew, Sunday was indeed a day of much-needed rest.

For those officers with special responsibilities there could be little immediate leisure, as their reports had to be prepared. Major Cooke and Lieutenants Harris, Durrant and Shotter had each to compile a separate report on their particular departments; Major Scott had to make his own comments and General Maitland, as the senior officer, had also to contribute some remarks. All of them had criticisms to make, explicitly or implicitly, for they knew that their views would help to frame official future policy towards airship development. Shotter, perhaps because of his junior rank, was surprisingly uncritical about the engines. Beyond the poor synchronisation of the two in the rear car, he found only minor points of which to complain. Scott and Maitland were both more outspoken on the defects of the Sunbeam Maoris; Scott considered them to be unsuitable and a source of great strain to the engineers, while Maitland declared the ship to be underpowered because of their inability to deliver more than half their theoretically possible revolutions. He believed their effective total horse-power was nearer 650 than the nominal 1,250. More speed, he insisted, was essential, and to help future flight-engineers, the possibility of bringing all the engines together in one place should be explored. The two senior officers also joined in urging more effective doping of the linen and the possible substitution of some stronger covering for the hull. Scott felt that the crew's quarters should be amidships in future designs, instead of forward, and he also wanted the hammocks replaced by lightweight beds in the bottom angles of the keel, to be safer, easier of access and not obstructive of the walking-way. One point on which he laid emphasis was the need to reduce the peculiar strains suffered by those taking part in long-distance flights. In particular, he suggested that a mechanical method of transferring the petrol would be much superior to the existing system of manual pumping.

Maitland added the weight of his opinion to the verdict of Cooke and Durrant that the new type of D.F.W.T. (Direction Finding Wireless Telegraphy) system was, as yet, virtually useless and required considerable development before it could be relied upon. He also supported Lieutenant Harris in his suggestion that far more information on weather conditions in the North Atlantic was urgently needed before transoceanic flights could become commonplace. Finally, he ended with a plea that the Medical Administrator should reverse his ruling concerning the official provision of rum aboard His Majesty's Airships.

All the reports were eventually handed to General Maitland for delivery to the Air Ministry. Together with a report from Major Pritchard, made separately to the Admiralty, they illustrate some of the contemporary problems of flying British dirigibles. It is also a comment upon the abortive nature of rigid airship development that few, if any, of the technical recommendations were ever satisfactorily implemented.

General Maitland had also been responsible for keeping a semi-official log of the voyage, of which the first part was handed to the Air Attaché in Washington, for delivery to the Press. Together with the latter half, it was printed, in full or in part, in many newspapers, and two years later was to be published in book form. Major Pritchard pointed out, amongst other things, that in sharp contrast to the Sunbeam engines, the Rolls Royce engines used by the earlier British rigids had not experienced a single breakdown in service.

On the Monday morning following the airship's return, three of R.34's officers: Maitland, Scott and, deservedly but rather surprisingly, Shotter, journeyed to London by train. At Liverpool Street Station they were met by a small deputation consisting of various officials, several senior R.A.F. officers, Mrs Winston Churchill and, most appropriately, General Masterman, the father of the Airship Service. Whether intentionally or no, the reception was marked by unpretentiousness and the small party were unrecognized and largely disregarded by the crowds of travellers and commuters. After handshakes all round, everyone drove off to the Air Ministry, where General Maitland gave a verbal account of the flight to his superiors and received their congratulations.

That meeting marked, in one sense, the signing-off of the whole venture. What followed could only be the postscript: an inevitable anti-climax for the men involved and a slow decline into forgetfulness by everyone else. Officers and men pretended, with perhaps genuine diffidence, that they had done only what any other of their service comrades could have performed equally well — each one, when interviewed, tried to place the credit elsewhere, usually on Major Scott. When Major Cooke was commended for his accurate navigation, he only remarked modestly that, 'America is six thousand miles long and it would have been surprising if we had not hit her!' His answer was typical of the crew's reaction to their brief hour of fame.

But the treatment accorded to all of them by officials, Press and public was oddly mixed.

The newspapers in Britain, as in the U.S.A., were convinced that the venture was literally epoch-making. Conditioned by the universally accepted analogy between airships and ocean liners, they believed that R.34 was the forerunner of vast dirigible fleets that would before long carry passengers and goods all over the world. Aeroplanes were generally dismissed as being too small for the commercial field and few people visualised that they would develop sufficiently to compete with airships over long distances. The shadow cast by Count Zeppelin obscured the way ahead and it is difficult for later generations, to whom rigid airships are extinct and dangerous monsters, to appreciate fully the extent to which they dominated contemporary public imagination. The *Illustrated London News*, for example, prefixed an article on an American troopship with the words, 'Before the days of the Transatlantic Dirigible', so managing to imply that such surface vessels were already outmoded. *The Times* editorial also waxed enthusiastic over R.34's achievement, which it compared more than favourably with that of Alcock and Brown. Rather unfairly, the leader-writer likened the former to a Great Northern express train and the latter to Dick Turpin! Even *Flight*, which might have possessed some extra degree of professional expertise, considered the exploit of Alcock and Brown more sporting than serious. R.34, it solemnly assured its readers, had accomplished what no aeroplane could perform and was the first of many commercial airships which would soon be plying an uneventful trade over the whole civilised globe. Other journals and newspapers took very much the same line and it is salutary to realise how the future of air travel was so completely misjudged and misinterpreted by almost everyone. Total disillusion with dirigibles lay only a decade in the future, but for the moment there was still an influential group of men in the Government whose attitude reflected general public opinion. After R.34's triumph, they were determined to press for the building of bigger and better airships.

The cause of this transitory optimism, R.34 herself, was soon on show to visitors, and the more privileged were taken round the ship in small parties. Apart from the engines and the damage sustained at Mineola, she was in good shape and only the worn and slack linen of the outer cover bore witness to seven thousand miles of travel. Not many days after arriving at Pulham she returned to East Fortune, although not by the direct route. Instead, she flew first to London, which was reached around seven o'clock in the evening. Keeping to a low altitude that her size might be the better seen and appreciated, she circled over the Houses of Parliament and the crowded streets of Westminster before moving off to the north. Her short time of glory was finally ended, for officials and crew alike predicted that within a very few years R.34 would be overtaken and made obsolete by larger, faster and more efficient successors.

Side by side with this misplaced technological optimism went a curious official neglect of the men who had produced it. Before very long, General Maitland and Major Scott were invited to Buckingham Palace to talk of their experiences. While King George V showed no more than polite interest in the voyage itself, he enquired particularly about the pigeons: a subject which always fascinated him. The newspapers, in reporting the royal audience, confidently predicted an early announcement of honours bestowed or rewards given — after all, both Sir John Alcock and Sir Arthur Whitten-Brown had won knighthoods for a lesser feat only weeks before. When the announcement came, however, it was surprisingly limited in both extent and degree. No knighthoods were given and such few awards as were distributed proved to be of comparatively minor value. There was little official recognition of the skill, endurance and bravery shown by the crew of the airship. Hindsight cannot diminish their achievement and for blazing a trail that millions have since followed, they

The memorial to R.34 at Mineola, Long Island. The plaque is identical to the one at East Fortune.
(Air League)

deserved better than they received. There was a banquet at the Royal Aero Club, a few other dinners and some public congratulation — but little else.

In retrospect, it is difficult to understand or to condone this strange neglect. General Maitland had become a C.M.G. earlier in the year and now, together with Major Cooke, Lieutenant Harris and Lieutenant Shotter, he was awarded the A.F.C. When one recalls the dubious activities which so often won knighthoods in that era, a medal seems a poor reward for such services as his. Major Scott fared only slightly better. He had won the A.F.C. during the war and to this only a C.B.E. was now added. It was his experience and knowledge that had brought R.34 safely through her long ordeal and yet his reward was small. He could reasonably have expected promotion but even this was inexplicably denied him. At least, he was not lost to aviation and after demobilisation in the autumn, he became Senior Flying Officer at Pulham, under the Civil Aviation Department.

If their captain was treated discourteously, the other crew members went largely unrewarded. Major Pritchard was later and separately awarded the A.F.C., but apart from the platinum cigarette cases presented to them by the United States Navy, the other officers received no official acknowledgement of their great exploit. Six of the warrant officers and N.C.O.s received the A.F.M. (Gent, Mayes, Robinson, Ripley, Scull and Watson), but the remainder gained nothing. Only one award appears to have found its way to the lower

78

ranks: the silver-mounted propelling pencils which had been presented to them by the New York Fire Brigade. As Corporal Burgess was overheard to remark, 'Six thousand miles for a bleeding pencil!' It seems a fair comment and those in authority evidently needed the reminder provided by George Robey. 'Do you know Arthur?' he asked a music hall audience. 'Arthur who?' they shouted back. 'R.34!' retorted the comedian triumphantly.

One member of the crew was alone in gaining something beyond his expectations and this, ironically, was Aircraftman William Ballantyne. Brought back to England with the R.A.F. ground-crew in the *Aquitania*, he should by rights have been court-martialled on a wide choice of charges. Instead, following Maitland's personal intervention, the case was quietly dropped and he escaped any punishment beyond being taken off flying duties for a time. A year later, probably owing to Major Scott's influence, he returned to airships and the extra two shillings a day flight-pay which they merited. At Howden he also met General Maitland again, who generously gave him a signed copy of his book, together with a mildly humorous reproof ('Here you are, naughty boy!') for the original misdeed.

In direct contrast to the British Government's lack of appreciation, the U.S. Naval Secretary went so far as to approve a recommendation that all the R.34 crew members should be granted Navy Crosses. The proposal was never implemented, however, as it was apparently considered that such an award would constitute a tactless diplomatic reproof.

Many years were to pass before any public monuments were set up to commemorate R.34's achievement. Not until 1957 was a bronze plaque unveiled at East Fortune, to be followed a year later by one at Mineola, and eventually, in 1989, by one at Pulham. While Alcock and Brown are names that most people know and recognize, the flight of the great airship has been forgotten far too easily and undeservedly. Even those who remember her do not always realize that she made the first direct aerial voyages between the United States and Britain; her aeroplane rival having only bridged the gap between Newfoundland and Ireland. Appropriately, therefore, if rather belatedly, a large model of R.34 was placed at London's Heathrow Airport in 1962. This was the most significant of her four memorials and it is the more saddening, therefore, that after some three decades, the model was removed from its position and is now on display in the Brooklands Museum.

One unusual tribute to the airship remained for some years, when the Watsonian Company developed a streamlined sidecar for motorcycles, which they named the 'R.34'. In more recent years, Liberia, Romania and the Comores have produced postage stamps bearing pictures of R.34, but neither she nor any other airship has ever appeared on a British stamp. In 1989, Coalport China produced a limited edition of 2,500 plates, designed by Melvin Buckley, depicting R.34 flying over North America. But there have been few other reminders of her achievement, although East Fortune aerodrome is now the home of the Scottish Museum of Flight, where are displayed relics of R.34, including her heraldic shield, photographs and a model.

If posterity has belittled the significance of her journey, one famous contemporary figure, at least, was in a unique position to appreciate the splendour of what R.34 had accomplished. Ten years before her voyage, Rudyard Kipling had written a short story called 'With the Night Mail' *(Actions and Reactions)*. This is a visionary account of a transatlantic aircraft of the future, which makes its landfall in the western hemisphere over Trinity Bay, just where the real airship had, in fact, first sighted land. A copy of the book was carried by R.34 and after the flight it was autographed by every member of the crew and presented to the author, who expressed his thanks with the rather less prophetic remark that he had 'always fancied the dirigible against the aeroplane for the overhead haulage of the years to come.'

Curiously, one item in the ship's stores had unexpectedly survived the peculiar hazards of the voyage and returned intact. Before the flight began, the Medical Officer at East Fortune, Surgeon Wedderburn, had packed a bottle of brandy with the medical kit. He was very surprised to find it still untouched on the airship's return and he took it back to keep as a souvenir. Seventy five years later it still exists — unopened and untasted.

The story of the transatlantic voyage concluded with unexpected news of the flight's only casualty. In the late afternoon of 11th July, the *S.S. West Kyska*, a tramp steamer of the Munson Line, was more than a thousand miles from port in Baltimore and around eight hundred miles away from New York when she was joined by the lost traveller. The female grey pigeon was heading straight towards Scotland, but with two-thirds of her impossible journey still to be covered, she landed exhausted on the ship's deck, as lucky as Harry Hawker and Kenneth Mackenzie-Grieve. Captain John Chapman picked her up and removed the ring on her leg to read the identification tag, N.U.R.P. 16-0. It meant nothing to him but until his ship reached port, the pigeon was petted, cosseted and closely guarded to prevent her from resuming her interrupted journey eastwards. On arrival in the United States she was identified as R.34's missing pigeon by Colonel Thwaite of the British Provost Guard. She provided a remarkable example of the homing instinct, as well as enabling the airship to retain her record of never losing a crew member, however humble.

CHAPTER 11

Ending

The Americans, no less than the British, were now fully convinced of the value of the large rigid dirigible. Developments in the United States moved almost parallel to the course they had taken in England and once again a wartime zeppelin was taken as the model for a local product. The German L.49 had come down in France in October 1917, and this time it was the Americans who made careful and detailed plans of her structure and design. In the first flush of enthusiasm engendered by R.34's visit, the United States Government decided to begin work on their own modified copy, which they designated ZR.1 (Zeppelin Rigid 1) and which later became the ill-fated *Shenandoah:* an Indian name meaning 'Daughter of the Stars'.

Both countries realised that the later German airships had advanced beyond the earlier design on which L.33 and L.49 were based. Since R.33 and R.34 were begun, further information had become available and the new fleet of airships which Britain proposed to build derived their inspiration, if not their exact design, from the 'long range' L.70 class. The fore-runner of these was R.38, on which work had already started and which the Americans had agreed to buy, at a cost of two million dollars. After delivery, she was to be renamed ZR.2 and to be commissioned before her theoretical predecessor, ZR.1. Many of her future crew were sent to England beforehand, in order to receive special training from the R.A.F. experts and to acquire experience in handling rigid airships, mainly with R.32. In 1920, they came to Howden airship station, where Maitland, now that the old Army style ranks had been abandoned, was an Air Commodore and the commanding officer. Lieutenant Charles Little of the C.5 blimp was among the American airmen and he was only one of several who were no strangers to the Britons.

Another old friend was stationed with them at Howden, although no longer the centre of attraction she had been during her hour of fame. R.34 had been officially returned to the Admiralty after her epic voyage, but she had actually been retained for training purposes by the R.A.F., to whom all airships were transferred in October, anyway. Since her return to East Fortune in July 1919, R.34 had spent more than six months being refitted, and not until February 1920 had she flown again, when she made the seven and a half hour flight to Pulham. Here she had remained grounded for six weeks before being permanently assigned to Howden, where she arrived at the end of March. From October 1919 until the middle of January 1921, her captain was William Hicks, now holding the new rank of Squadron Leader. Like her sister ship, R.34 was virtually obsolete, but until their replacements were ready to take over, they were both to continue in service. Of this, however, there was soon considerable doubt, for official attitudes were changing. The building of R.38 took longer than had been expected and the prospective cost of more large airships was beginning to daunt the British Government, obsessed by the need for peacetime economy. There were

R.33 fastened to the mooring mast at Pulham in 1921. It was this mast which might have saved R.34 a few months earlier. (Imperial War Museum)

other reasons, too. When the Royal Air Force was formed by amalgamating the Royal Naval Air Service with the Royal Flying Corps in 1918, it was the latter body which dominated the new organization. Unlike the officials of the Admiralty, those at the Air Ministry, particularly Hugh Trenchard, had little experience or appreciation of airships, and the large fleet in service at the time of the Armistice was drastically reduced until by late 1920 only two non-rigids were left and only four rigids: R.32, R.33, R.34 and R.80, the last of which had only just been delivered. Three other rigids had been ordered, but of these, only R.36 was delivered during the following year. The other two were R.35 and R.37, both of which were cancelled before completion, for there was increasing pressure to relegate airships to civilian purposes, or even to discourage their use altogether. Although no announcement was made until early 1921, it is clear that preparations had been made some time before for dissolving the Airship Service as a specialist branch of the R.A.F.

During her stay at Howden, R.34 was modified to enable her to use a mooring-mast, of the type which was gradually being introduced. Her nose was suitably altered and in order to do this, the coat-of-arms at her bows was removed for the first time since leaving the factory at Inchinnan. The walking-way was extended to reach the nose, where a hatchway now led out to the mast. A cone was fitted to the centre of the nose, and this connected with the mast through a special coupling. No mooring-mast had, in fact, yet been erected at Howden, although one had recently been authorised, so the coupling was fitted instead to R.33, as this vessel was required for early experiments with the mast at Pulham. Another one was ordered for R.34, as a replacement, but this had still not arrived by the end of January 1921. If the loss of her figurehead was of no more than symbolic importance, the lack of mast and coupling was of greater consequence and may have fatally deprived the airship of a safe anchorage in a time of need.

On 27 January, just after midday, R.34 made ready to leave Howden on her first flight for several months, carrying an instructional crew of eight navigation officers. In addition to this training purpose, the intention was to check the ship after recent repairs and especially to test the efficiency of the automatic gas-valves. Many changes had taken place in the crew over the past eighteen months through demobilisation or promotion; Flying-Officer Harold Luck was now Second Officer and the captain, with the rank of Flight-Lieutenant, was Hedley V. Drew. Although a capable officer with a successful career ahead of him, he was at this time a young man without the long experience of either of his predecessors. He had taken over command of R.34 only six days previously and so was not entirely to blame for the mistakes which had already made straight the way towards disaster.

Only the charts which had been issued to the airship before the Atlantic flight were on board, and it is clear that they were now out of date and that mistakes would therefore be made in identifying the lights, lightships and lightbuoys. Because the new captain was unfamiliar with the coast over which he was about to cruise, he was unable either to appreciate or to rectify these errors. To all appearances, the wireless apparatus upon which so much depended — both for communication and for direction finding — was in good order and had been inspected only a day or so earlier. In reality, one small but crucial fault had been overlooked, for a defective wavemeter meant that messages sent out by the ship's W.T. operators were transmitted on an incorrect wavelength. Compounding this oversight was an extraordinary confusion over the ship's call-sign — the means by which messages to a particular vessel were separated and distinguished among the numerous transmissions from base. On the previous flight, the call-sign for R.34 had been D.M.D. but although this no longer applied, no one in the airship had been informed of the change. While the ship was ascending slowly from the airfield, the senior W.T. operator on board contacted the ground by Aldis signal lamp and was told that the correct call-sign was now 7 V K. In reality, it was 7 V F and the duty signaller below only found out and reported his mistake much later, when the harm had already been done.

In the meantime, this chain of errors remained undiscovered as the airship circled the field and completed the preliminary tests before moving off towards Hull, Spurn Head and the North Sea in clear conditions and with a light wind from the north-north-east. For some time thereafter, in an ironic interplay of human misunderstanding and mechanical failure, the messages from Howden to R.34 went unrecognized, while those from the airship to base were directed astray, through being transmitted on the wrong wavelength. When the ship's operators found their own signals went unanswered, they at first drew the erroneous conclusion that it was Howden's receivers which were at fault, rather than their own transmitters. Even when they eventually realised that the wavemeter was broken and that they were tuned incorrectly, they assumed that the actual discrepancy was small and they altered the wavelength of their transmissions only slightly each time, in the hope of being soon received. Back on the airfield, there was no immediate concern over the failure of communications, and it was nearly four o'clock before Air Commodore Maitland was told there was no contact with the airship. He at once ordered that R.34 should be recalled and that the message should be repeated at intervals until understood.

By this time, the airship was well out to sea and the order to return, duly received and recorded, was assumed by both the operators and the captain to be directed at another airship, the wooden-framed R.32, which was also out on a training flight. Not until an hour later, when the message was again received, did they begin to suspect what had really happened and Flight-Lieutenant Drew immediately decided to turn the ship and return to base, steering a course north-westward. His suspicions were confirmed some time afterwards when a message was intercepted showing that R.32 was just landing and so could not have required the earlier recall signals. Meanwhile, the ship's operators had tried transmitting by 'spark', a more primitive method but one which covered a wider range of wavelengths, and they were picked up by the wireless operators at the Flamborough station. These then passed on a message to Howden, requesting that a wide search of wavebands be made. This resulted in contact being at last established with the base, at half past seven, when the airship was found to be transmitting on 2030 metres, instead of the regulation 1300.

At around the same time, from a height of about 2,700 ft, lights were sighted several miles away on either side of the airship, and these were identified by the captain as the Inner Dowsing and the Outer Dowsing, some thirty miles or so to the south-east and east of the mouth of the Humber. A flashing light was also seen in the distance on the starboard bow and after reference to the charts and the light list, this was taken by Drew to be the lighthouse on Spurn Head. He informed Howden of his position and maintained the ship's course for home in gradually worsening weather, at an airspeed of about 48 m.p.h. A short while earlier, he had ordered all the engines briefly to full power, in an attempt to find the ship's maximum speed, and this was registered as between 47 and 49 knots (54 − 56 m.p.h.).

As captain of the ship, Drew alone was responsible for navigation and he could not officially delegate this duty, even to the eight qualified navigators whom he was carrying. Nevertheless, a tacit agreement seems to have been reached and the calculations of these officers were largely responsible for determining the course taken by R.34 after Drew handed over command to Flying-Officer Luck at eight o'clock. Secure in the assurance that R.34 was safely on course for home, Drew retired to his hammock in the keel, after leaving orders that he was to be informed when the mainland was reached.

Forty minutes later, when R.34 crossed the coast, the sky had become heavily overcast and patches of low-lying cloud blotted out much of the ground below. For some time now, there had been a changing and strengthening of the wind, which had swung round to blow from the south-west. Although this had been forecast earlier, the navigators seem to have been unaware that the airship had been pushed so far northwards and when a flashing light was seen on the port beam, Luck was told by Squadron-Leader Gaskell, one of the navigation officers, that the ship was now over the Humber and about two miles from Spurn Head. Undoubtedly, however, it was the coast just beyond Flamborough Head, some forty miles further north, where there was another lighthouse, that was actually their landfall and Luck was unwise enough to accept this wrong judgement without making any attempt at verification. He informed the captain that the coast had been passed, but Drew in his turn also failed to check the ship's position for himself and he remained in his hammock after giving orders for the course to be altered appropriately. At about the same time a belated endeavour was made to check the amount of drift the ship was making, but she was pitching and yawing too much for any accurate result to be obtained. Twice more the course was altered before Drew came back to the control-cabin at about five past ten, to be told that a further order had been received from Howden, once again ordering him to return as soon as possible. During the time he had been resting, the weather conditions had deteriorated sharply, with thickening low cloud and rain adding to the difficulties of navigation. The ship's position was now thought to be somewhere south-west of Flamborough Head: a supposition which still appeared probable to Drew, even when the blast furnaces of a unknown town emerged from the gloom to glow dully beneath the airship's keel.

More puzzled than disconcerted by this unexpected sight of what was later reckoned to have been Redcar, Drew then brought R.34 down through the clouds to a height of only 1,200 ft, from where it was possible to discern high ground less than 400 ft below. There was no sign of the sea and no recognizable landmark, so he ordered the ship up to a safe height again and continued on his previous course, still reasonably confident of his whereabouts. At half past eleven a wireless bearing was obtained from Flamborough, which appeared to indicate that the ship was way out over the North Sea. As such bearings were frequently inaccurate over very short distances, and as there was clearly land below the airship, this was dismissed as impossible. However, all bearings could be read in exactly the opposite direction and the back bearing gave the ship a position somewhere among the hills of north Yorkshire. Nevertheless, none of the navigators could believe she was so far from the position they had calculated and the warning went unheeded.

Towards midnight, with clouds hemming in the airship above and below, and with rain and stiff winds buffeting her, Drew once again ordered R.34 down to a height of 1,200 ft. While he was beginning to distrust the navigators' calculations, he had yet no idea that the divergence between reality and supposition was so great. Still believing the ship to be over the comparatively flat countryside of the Wolds, he hoped to break through the clouds and find some landmark which would enable him to obtain a firm position. He left Luck in the control-cabin and went himself into the wireless cabin, where the operators were trying to get a fresh bearing from Flamborough. By now he had decided that if the airship's location could not be established with certainty, he would return to the coast and wait for daylight and an improvement in the weather before again trying to reach Howden.

At midnight the watch was changed and the men going off duty climbed into their sleeping bags to snatch four hours' sleep. One of them, Aircraftman Johnson, delayed a few minutes to drink some cocoa before he also swung himself into his hammock. Just as he did so, the airship gave a violent shudder and there came a harsh grinding sound as the forward and after cars scraped over rough moorland. The lights in the control-cabin failed, men were sent sprawling and there was momentary confusion and panic. At ten minutes past twelve exactly, a sudden downdraught had caught R.34 and pushed her into an unseen slope: probably somewhere near Guisborough Moor in the Cleveland Hills. Mercifully, the hill was low and the ship struck only lightly before lurching clear again. Luck immediately rang to stop the engines and the ship was at once carried away helplessly by the wind, like a piece of airborne flotsam. Ballast was dropped to lift her to a safer height and while lighting was being restored to the control-cabin, the amount of damage was hastily assessed. It was found to be surprisingly little; clumps of heather were stuck to the control-car and some windows smashed, the bumping-bags had been carried off, one girder in the keel was twisted, two engine-car struts damaged, the wireless aerial shortened and the fore and aft propellers reduced to stubs.

Only this last was of serious moment, for the ship was deprived of more than half of her already inadequate power. Once the full extent of the harm was realised, the two wing engines were restarted and they fought stubbornly against the ebbing tide of the winds that were sweeping the airship out over the North Sea again. At medium power, the thrust of the Sunbeams was inadequate and only by constant use of full power was it possible for Drew to check the seawards drift. For the first time, perhaps, the engines proved equal to the demands made upon them and they ran at top speed without faltering and without failure. Now reaching speeds of up to 30 m.p.h. at 1,500 ft and above, the wind weakened somewhat towards sea-level and blew from a slightly more favourable direction. Drew took R.34 down as low as was safely possible and headed her westwards again. By regularly valving gas and maintaining an altitude of around 500 ft, the worst violence of the gale was avoided and the airship crept laboriously forward. The possibility of seeking refuge at Pulham was briefly considered, but deprived as she was of the vital coupling at her nose, R.34 could not have used the mooring-mast there and so Drew decided to continue towards Howden.

Soon the aerial was lengthened by a strand of spare copper wire that was found in the keel, and the wireless operators were able to regain contact with the base. With daylight, the true position of the airship was established and Maitland arranged for two destroyers to be sent out from Harwich and a tug from Hull, but there was little else that could be done except to await events and send out regular weather reports. All through that Friday, the crippled R.34 limped slowly homewards, butting her bows doggedly into the wind and dipping unsteadily as the two engines strained to their limits. At midday she was near the mouth of the Humber and crawling towards Hull, which she reached at about one o'clock. Although now only twenty miles or so from Howden, she took more than three hours to cover this final, painful lap and it was in the early darkness of a winter's day that the airship struggled in to her last, sad landing. Still contending against the fierce wind, she descended slowly into the hands of the four hundred men of the landing-party, who led her, rolling and pitching, towards the safety of the hangar. They managed to haul her almost within reach of the doors, but because of the boisterous and uncertain wind, it proved impossible to manoeuvre her into a position where she could enter. The hangar's vast bulk and the nearby screens caused strong and erratic eddies to tilt and twist the ship almost beyond control, and vicious squalls repeatedly lifted her up and then dashed her down to earth again. During one of these gusts, the after car was swung 60 ft off the ground, with some of the landing-party still hanging on to it, while others fought to prevent the airship from breaking away altogether. More damage was done to the forward and after cars, the rudder jammed hard over and the controls became inoperative. Finally, Maitland gave the order to abandon ship and when all the crew had scrambled safely to the ground, the stricken vessel was led back to the mooring block to be perforce anchored by the same three-wire system which had proved adequate at Mineola, although this method had never before been employed at Howden and the airmen there were inexperienced in its use.

In the confusion of rain, squall and darkness, further damage was done; the forward gasbags were punctured by a broken girder and the gas valves may have been opened when the forward car became partly detached from the hull. Eventually, however, the airship was tethered to the block and there the exhausted airmen left her, tugging and plunging at the hawsers that held her down. To all appearances she was now safe until a return to calm weather should allow her to be housed and repaired. It was not to be. During a night of continuing storm, the ship settled into the ground, her bows were smashed and the once stately vessel reduced to a ravaged hulk. In the chill light of the next morning it was obvious that R.34 would never fly again. So complete was her destruction and so far was she beyond repair, that within three or four days her carcase had been dismembered by gangs of workmen. The fabric was stripped off, the remaining equipment removed and the framework chopped up with axes to be sold for its value as scrap metal.

One generous gesture was made by Flight-Lieutenant Drew, which was understood and appreciated by those to whom it was addressed. On the morning after R.34's destruction he appeared briefly in the lower ranks' barrack room and apologised for what had occurred. His responsibility was only partial, for ironies, contradictions and confusions abound in this last chapter of R.34's story. Eight extra navigators were on board, yet she lost her way. The defective wavemeter should have compelled her to return to base, yet this chance was lost because of a wrong call-sign. She might have found safety at the Pulham mooring-mast, yet the lack of a coupling made this impracticable. A wireless bearing gave warning of the dangers below, but was disregarded by officers unwilling to accept that their own calculations might be faulty.

By a final irony, the Court of Inquiry which investigated the whole episode included the navigator of the Atlantic, Squadron-Leader G. G. H. Cooke. Confronted by the evidence of such diverse errors, its four members found it impossible to declare any one individual to blame for the loss of the airship. Instead, they were obliged to criticise the Station Wireless Officer, Flying-Officer Wicks and even Squadron-Leader Gaskell, as well as Flight-Lieutenant Drew and Flying-Officer Luck. In mitigation, they found that Drew had displayed great skill in bringing his ship back to base and that his errors were those of inexperience.

When their report reached the Air Ministry, the guilt was placed by the Air Council on Drew and on those senior officers whose unpleasant privilege it was to take responsibility for the faults of their subordinates. Characteristically, Maitland had greeted Drew on his safe return to Howden only by congratulating him on his excellent landing, and now he was joined by the Senior Flying Officer, Flight-Lieutenant Wann, and by Drew himself in receiving a reprimand. Undoubtedly, it was the unpredictable and severe weather which was largely to blame for the ship's destruction and the Air Council stated flatly that the flight should never have been undertaken. Typically, they ignored the expert testimony of the Meteorological Officer at Howden that such atrocious weather could not have been foreseen. No publicity was given to the Court of Inquiry and as its findings were not divulged, the whole matter was treated cursorily by the newspapers and soon forgotten. Despite her financial value, R.34's design was now some five years old and she could have had little further to contribute to future developments in aviation. For this reason, perhaps, and also because nobody had been injured, comparatively little concern was expressed over her fate.

She was a ship that had always inspired respect and affection in those who had dealings with her. She was the cause of no loss of life or property and her one great exploit gave pride and pleasure to many. To those who had flown to the United States and back, her passing was especially a matter of regret. But it went deeper than this, and although the comments of Air Commodore Maitland and Major Scott are not recorded, they could not have known that the disappearance of 'Tiny' was of more than sentimental interest. She showed, in fact, the shape of future events. For another twenty years, rigid airships continued to be built and flown in Britain, Germany and the United States. In the last half century since then, there has been not one.

Britain's last two rigid airships: R.100 and R.101

CHAPTER 12

Aftermath

Two decades after the loss of R.34, she was followed into oblivion by the last of her successors, and it can almost be said that the last act of the rigid airship drama was signalled by the exit of R.34 from the stage. In Britain during 1921, R.32 and R.80 were deleted, as were the last two non-rigids. Only R.33 and R.36 remained in service, the latter registered from the first as a civilian aircraft. Both survived for some years, but no airship has since been used by the British armed forces.

By the middle months of 1921, R.38 was completed and made ready for her trials. Although based on German practice, she was not a straightforward copy, as was R.34, and she had been designed by the staff of government officials attached to the Air Ministry. They had planned the new ship entirely on empirical lines, copying the sizes of the girders in the zeppelins, but without making any scientific calculations of the aerodynamic stresses involved. At great heights, where the later German airships were intended to operate, the strain imposed on an aircraft's structure by sharp manoeuvring is considerably less than at low altitudes, because of the decreased air-pressure. The British designers apparently ignored this necessity of reconciling the separate needs of handling and lightness, and their new airship, unlike the zeppelins, had controls which permitted sudden and violent changes of course. In her time, R.38 was the largest aircraft ever built, for although rather shorter than L.72, a bigger diameter gave her a capacity of 2,700,000 cubic ft, slightly more than her German counterpart. Beautiful in form and impressive in concept, she was soon found to have little of the tractability or steadiness of her predecessors. During her first, brief flights there appeared ominous structural damage caused by aerodynamic strains and large sections of girders had to be replaced. Flight-Lieutenant J. E. M. Pritchard, who had reverted to his substantive rank, was the acceptance officer for the trial flights and he submitted a report urging the need for prolonged and careful testing. His recommendations were disregarded, for the Americans, conscious of several months' delay, were anxious to take the ship home as soon as possible and Maitland, now in overall charge, was compelled to move faster than he would have wished.

Tuesday, 23 August, was chosen for the final trial and pre-delivery flight, and R.38 left Howden in the early morning under the command of Flight-Lieutenant Wann. The intention was to carry out a long, proving flight over the North Sea and then to proceed to Pulham, where the airship would be handed over to the Americans for them to fly her home. That day passed without a hitch, the ship steering, handling and performing to nearly everyone's satisfaction, but when fog obscured the approach to Pulham, it was decided to return to Howden, where arrangements were made for the ship to be docked at half-past six on the Wednesday evening.

The base was reached with time and fuel to spare, so as a final speed test, the ship turned

R.38, which 'failed and fell', as the memorial plaque records. (Airship Heritage Trust)

back towards Hull, over which she circled in the late afternoon. Again, all went well and at 1,500 ft above the Humber, R.38 headed for Howden and the end of the two-day journey. The last turn was being completed and the speed reduced, when suddenly there came the sharp screech of girders and wires snapping violently asunder. A hole, clearly visible from the ground, opened up in the underside of the airship and grew rapidly wider to become a yawning gap; within a matter of only seconds, the ship had broken clean in two. The forward section tumbled headlong towards the river, trailing clouds of black smoke as petrol and hydrogen burst into shimmering flame. There was nothing that could be done to save the ship and little time even for men to save themselves. From the wireless-cabin came one last despairing message, picked up at Howden: 'Ship broken; falling'. The operator had time for no more and he became one of the 44 men who perished; five only came out alive. Three of these descended on the tip of the tail, their fall cushioned by the fins, and one more was picked up from the water just in front of them. Rescuers who tried to approach the forward car were held off by burning oil until it sank beneath the surface. Only at the last moment did someone manage to force his boat through a gap in the flames and pull two men from the wreckage. One was Lieutenant Little, who died almost immediately, and the other was Flight-Lieutenant Wann, injured but alive.

Among the dead were Jack Pritchard and Edward Maitland. Both appear to have been in the control-cabin during the last minutes before the crash and both might well have saved themselves by using one of the parachutes stacked everywhere in readiness. Maitland had parachuted from airships more often than any other man but he stayed in the cabin to the end, trying desperately and selflessly to check the ship's rapid descent. When his body was eventually recovered, his hand was found to be still locked in a death-grip on the toggles that released the water-ballast. His end was typical of his whole life, for he never left others to brave a danger alone. With his death there was lost England's strongest advocate for the continued use of rigid airships, in peace as well as in war, and his plans for an extended commercial programme were never realised. Two others who died had also been connected with R.34: C.I.R. Campbell had drawn up her plans, and Aircraftman Roy Parker had flown the Atlantic aboard her.

The years ahead were to show a nearly unbroken record of rigid airship disasters, with one or two successes failing to relieve a picture of almost uniform failure. In Britain, R.33 made a spectacular recovery when blown away across the North Sea, while R.36 was scrapped after some years lying idle. In 1928, R.33 was finally declared obsolete and broken up — a dozen years after the capture and copying of L.33. For a short while only, the Air Ministry resumed its interest in dirigibles and in 1924 the Government sponsored the construction of R.101, in virtual competition with R.100, an airship whose support came from industry. With a length of 777 ft and a capacity of 5,500,000 cubic ft, R.101 was in her turn the largest aircraft in the world, but in October 1930, on her way to India, she burst into flames on a French hillside, killing forty eight of the fifty four people on board. Two of those who died were former members of R.34's crew — Major G.H. Scott and W.R. Gent. This second disaster brought an end to all airship building in Britain for nearly half a century. R.100, despite her great promise and a near-faultless flight to Canada and back, was immediately grounded and eventually sold for scrap metal — the last of the seventeen rigid airships built in Britain.

Across the Atlantic, a similar although more prolonged process took shape. Four years after the R.38 disaster, *Shenandoah* was lost, together with fourteen of her forty three crew-members, despite using the safe helium gas. Her captain, who perished with his ship, was the same Zachary Lansdowne who had accompanied R.34 on her outward journey to New York. Six years later, *Akron* was built — 785 ft long and of 6,500,000 cubic ft capacity. Her sister ship, *Macon*, followed two years later, in 1933. Both dirigibles used helium and both crashed to destruction in the sea: the former in 1933 when seventy four of her seventy seven crew were killed, and the latter in 1935, when only two out of eighty one died. After *Macon*, no more rigid airships were made in the United States, although the American monopoly of helium allowed many small non-rigids to be flown successfully and safely throughout the Second World War and after. The most advanced of these were the four blimps of the ZPG-3W class, 403 ft long and with a capacity of 1,500,000 cubic ft. They were the largest and fastest non-rigid airships ever made and the first flew in 1958.

As the numbers of disasters steadily increased during the years between the wars, other countries lost faith in the airship. In France, the confiscated L.72 was renamed *Dixmude* and made several fine flights for her new masters, including one which broke R.34's world endurance record. Then in December 1923, she crashed into the Mediterranean with the loss of all on board.

Italy continued to build semi-rigid airships and *Norge* became famous for her flight over the North Pole in 1926. Two years later, her sister ship, *Italia,* crashed in the Arctic with the loss of several lives, so bringing an end to Italian airship development.

Germany was the last country to maintain interest in the rigid airship, but the two rigids built after the Armistice were confiscated following the Treaty of Versailles, as were the remaining wartime ships. One rigid, known eventually as *Los Angeles,* was made for the

United States as part of the war reparations, but it was not until 1928 that the Zeppelin Company managed to make the first rigid airship to be retained in Germany since the war. Officially known as LZ.127, it was as *Graf Zeppelin* that she became, without question, the most famous airship of all time. She was 775 ft long, had a total capacity of 3,700.000 cubic feet and was one of the most beautiful of all man-made objects. More than half a century later, at least one elderly man has a childhood memory of her silver-grey slenderness moving gracefully above the distant ocean horizon.

For a decade, the *Graf Zeppelin* wandered through the skies, setting innumerable records and carrying freight or passengers in comfort and safety. She became the only airship ever to fly round the world, she crossed the Atlantic more than a hundred times and she covered more than a million miles without losing a life. In 1936, her successor was launched as LZ.129 or *Hindenburg* and was the largest flying machine ever. She was 803 ft long, had a maximum diameter of 135 ft and a capacity of 7,000,000 cubic ft — three and a half times that of R.34. She boasted accommodation with a standard of comfort and luxury never attained since by any airship or aeroplane. But the Americans had refused to supply helium and on 6 May 1937, coming in to land at New Jersey, *Hindenburg* suddenly and inexplicably burst into flames and within a few minutes was totally destroyed. Of the ninety seven people on board, sixty two miraculously got out alive. All the rest, comprising twenty two crew-members and thirteen passengers, were killed. The disaster was officially attributed to static electricity, but this was only one of many theories. It was the end not only of *Hindenburg*, but of all rigid airships. The *Graf Zeppelin* was taken out of service immediately and scrapped three years later. A sister ship of *Hindenburg*, confusingly also called *Graf Zeppelin*, was completed and flew briefly before the war, but she also was scrapped in 1940. Since then, no large rigid airship of the traditional form has ever flown.

During the Second World War and for many years afterwards, the Americans continued to employ military airships, but when the last of these flew in 1962, only the few small blimps maintained for publicity purposes by the Goodyear Company remained. The poor safety record of airships during the first half of the twentieth century could not be forgotten, although the three factors of bad design, poor weather forecasting and inflammable gas, which had caused the disasters, no longer applied. It seemed that airships, despite their obvious qualities and the increased availability of helium, would finally disappear completely.

But in the last three decades of the twentieth century there has been a remarkable resurgence of interest in airships. All over the world, new types of non-rigids have appeared, basically similar to their predecessors, but safer and much more sophisticated. The use of helium allows the car to be fitted directly to the envelope, with the rigging lines positioned internally. In Britain, Airship Industries were for many years very successful manufacturers, until their parent company failed. In the decade following 1979 they built fifteen airships, of which six were sold to other firms. These were either the Skyship 500, with a length of 171 ft and a capacity of 182,000 cubic ft, or the Skyship 600, with a length of 194 ft and a capacity of 235,000 cubic ft. They are scientifically designed, make use of the latest materials and, in common with some early British airships, they use swivelling propellers to provide vectored thrust, so pushing the blimp up or down as required. This ability makes for safer landing and take-off, as well as reducing the number of handlers required and helping to conserve valuable helium. These small airships have proved to be comfortable, quiet and safe. They have been used for fishery patrols, tourist flights, advertising and other duties.

From Britain, also, have come the airships of Thunder and Colt, of Shropshire. These are made to order and include blimps using hot air for lift, instead of gas. One of their craft, the AS 261, was the world's biggest ever hot-air dirigible and was used to help scientists surveying the forest canopy of the Amazon.

Another manufacturer of hot-air blimps is Cameron Balloons of Bristol, which also makes to order the world's smallest ever helium airship. This, the DG 14, is only 62 ft long and has a capacity of 14,000 cubic ft.

Other countries have also produced airships, or are in the process of designing them. China and Canada, as well as the United States, have flown their own designs and in Germany the Zeppelin Company is considering the possibility of a new rigid airship. In Costa Rica there is activity, in Russia an innovative new design has appeared, and in Mexico a novel form of small rigid airship has been built and flown. Unfortunately, the world-wide recession is hampering progress and many projects for the introduction of more unorthodox forms have had to be shelved, for lack of money. Yet the virtues of the airship, in particular its ability to remain aloft for days at a time, make it particularly suitable for many purposes. For coastguard duties, especially to watch for drug smugglers, the airship would possess many advantages over aeroplanes and helicopters. Airships of a shallow, broad configuration produce considerable dynamic lift and would make excellent transoceanic cargo carriers, taking goods direct from the manufacturer in one country to the retail outlet in another, so saving the expense and bother of lorries, shipping and lorries again on the other side. For touring and sightseeing, the comfort and visibility of airship passenger accommodation is incomparably better than the cramped seating of airliners. For aerial surveying and the televising of sporting events, the steady platform of the airship is well-suited. For the transport of heavy or bulky objects, the airship can be combined with the helicopter to make a hybrid aerial crane.

In the summer of 1993, it was announced by the Ministry of Defence that a Skyship blimp was being evaluated for use by the Army in Northern Ireland. If trials prove satisfactory, four such airships may be used for surveillance work and the co-ordination of anti-terrorist operations. Apart from being more economical than helicopters, they possess much greater endurance and carrying capacity, are quieter and less obtrusive, and are probably safer. These could be the first airships operated by the armed forces of Britain for more than seventy years.

Airships, it would seem, now have a future as well as a past. R.34, for so long forgotten, may one day be famous not as the embodiment of a failed and obsolete method of transport, but as a pioneer and innovator.

Bibliography

Abbott, Patrick	The British Airship at War 1914 – 1918, 1989
Allen, Peter	The 91 before Lindbergh, 1984
Clarke, Basil	The History of Airships, 1961
Davy, M. J. B.	Interpretive History of Flight, 1948
Durand, W. F.	Aerodynamic Theory, 1934
Gunston, Bill	World Encyclopedia of Aero Engines, 1987
Harrison, Michael	Airborne at Kittyhawk, 1953
Higham, Robin	The British Rigid Airship 1908 – 1931, 1962
Jackson, Robert	Airships, 1971
Janes	All the World's Aircraft, 1919
Lehmann, E. A. & Mingos, H.	The Zeppelins, 1927
Maitland, Edward	Log of H.M.A.R.34, 1921
Meager, George	My Airship Flights, 1915 – 1930, 1970
Norris, G.	The Royal Flying Corps, 1965
Poolman, Kenneth	Zeppelins over England, 1960
Raleigh, W. & Jones, H. A.	War in the Air, 1928
Robinson, Douglas	The Zeppelin in Combat, 1962
Shute, Nevil	Slide Rule, 1954
Sinclair, J. A.	Airships in Peace and War, 1934
Toland, J.	Ships in the Sky, 1957
Vaeth, G.	Graf Zeppelin, 1959
White, William J.	Airships for the Future, 1976
Wykes, A.	Air Atlantic, 1967

Sources

Public Record Office:

Transatlantic Flight of R.34. Air 1/110/1338
History and Record of Airships. Air 1/2315/222/6/A
Proceedings of Court of Inquiry into loss of R.34. Air 2/207/70200/21

Science Museum:

Report to Admiralty on Atlantic flight — J.E.M. Pritchard.
Report to Admiralty on last flight — J.E.M. Pritchard.

Royal Aeronautical Society Library:

The Maitland papers, including the diary of Lieutenant Luck.
Rigid airships and mooring gear — Admiralty File 1918.
The Atlantic Flight of H.M. Airship R.34 by E. E.Turner — Paper of a lecture to the
Society of Engineers in 1922.
Contemporary accounts of R.34 in many newspapers, both English and American, from
an album of cuttings compiled for the R.Ae.S. in 1919.
The Newman Alcock papers.

Miscellaneous:

Article about Ballantyne in Sunday Express, 29 June 1969.
Experiments on Rigid Airship R.33 — H.M.S.O 1921.
Notes on R.34's second trial flight, from a document in the possession of Lord Ventry.
Scott of the Atlantic by E. A. Johnston — article in *Dirigible,* July – September 1989.
The Flight of the R.34 by William K. Kaiser — article in *The Hofstra Review,* Autumn
1969.
Extract from R.34's log book, of unknown provenance.
Contemporary letter from crew-member, describing loss of R.34.

Periodicals:

*Flight, Aeroplane, Aeronautics, Engineering, Illustrated London News, The Times,
Glasgow Bulletin, Airship (*The magazine of the Airship Association), *Dirigible* (The
magazine of the Friends of Cardington Airship Station).

Personal Recollections:

The following have all provided facts or anecdotes from their own experience.

Mrs. H. Pritchard — widow of Major J. E. M. Pritchard.
Mrs. O. O'Riordan — formerly engaged to Captain Greenland.
Major-General J.Shotter — crew member R.34.
Mr. F. P. Browdie — crew member R.34.
Squadron-Leader J. Forteath — crew member R.34.
Flight-Lieutenant W. W. Ballantyne — crew member R.34.
Mr. W. Johnson — crew member R.34 and R.38.
Captain T. B. Williams — ground crew, Pulham.
Mr. H. Howe-Double — ground crew, East Fortune.

Flights of R.34

From	To	Dates	Duration (Hours)	Details
Inchinnan	Inchinnan	14 March 1919	5	First Trial
Inchinnan	Inchinnan	24 – 25 March	19	Second Trial
Inchinnan	East Fortune	28 – 29 May	21	Third Trial & Acceptance
East Fortune	East Fortune	15 – 16 June	6	Training
East Fortune	East Fortune	17 – 20 June	56	Baltic flight
East Fortune	New York	2 – 6 July	108	Atlantic flight
New York	Pulham	9 – 13 July	75	Atlantic flight
Pulham	East Fortune	31 July – 1 Aug.	13	London and base
East Fortune	Pulham	4 – 5 Feb. 1920	8	Change of base
Pulham	Howden	20 March 1920	14	Change of base
Howden	Howden	27 – 28 Jan. 1921	28	Last flight
			353 hours	

INDEX